DATE DUE

DEMCO, INC. 38-2931

PRINTED IN U.S.A.

44062

RUG MAKING
Techniques and Design

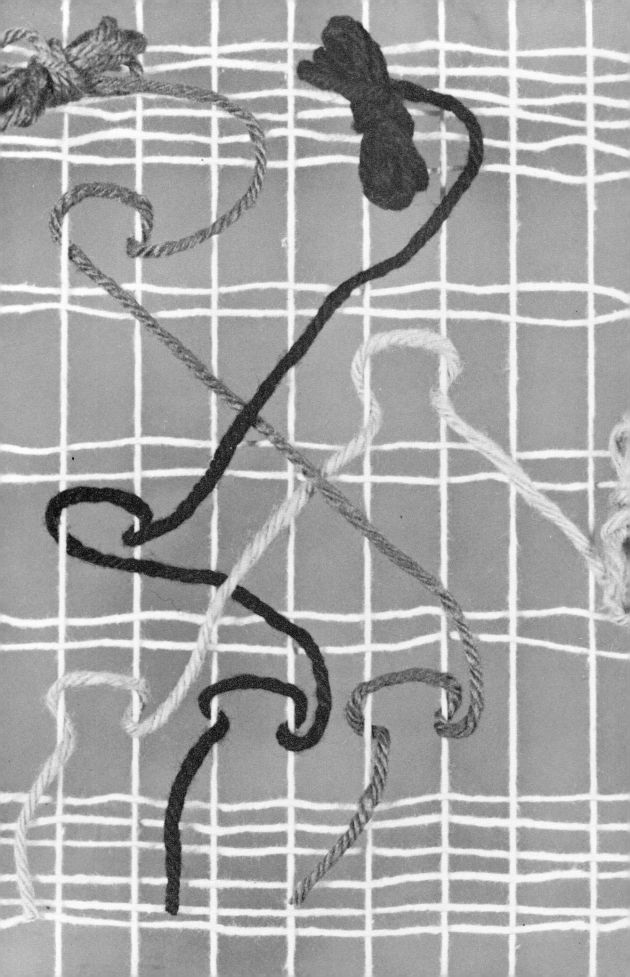

MARY ALLARD

RUG MAKING
Techniques and Design

CHILTON BOOKS

A DIVISION OF CHILTON COMPANY

Publishers

Philadelphia   New York

All photographs by Lou Thurrott
unless credited otherwise
Designed by William E. Lickfield
Manufactured in the United States of America by
Quinn & Boden Company, Inc., Rahway, N. J.

Preface

IS HANDMAKING A RUG FOR THE ELECT?

There are two major parts to the making of any rug. One, the **labor**—the actual fashioning of the rug, the manual process or technique of bringing it into being. The other, the **designing**—the use to which the labor is put, the idea that is to be translated into rug form.

The first, the actual making of the rug, is quite simple; so simple, in fact, that even the most artistically acclaimed, the Oriental, was made by small children. While it does not always follow that because an object is more spectacular it is more difficult to make than one that is less resplendent, it is true that no rug technique is particularly difficult. All processes for handmaking any kind of rug consist of few and relatively simple steps which can be learned within a short time. And they require little particular facility except wanting to make them. This does not mean that after a few hours one can expect to become a master—only practice and a thorough understanding of the craft will do that. But there is no reason why even the very first rug cannot be a very creditable job; as creditable as any subsequent rugs, though those will become increasingly easier and faster to make. Repetition and practice are bound to engender a freer and faster use of techniques.

The second aspect of the rug-making process—how to use those easily learned techniques, the designing of the rug—is not so much less simple as it is less tangible. It is a more creative and more elusive process that does not lend itself so readily to definition. Once a technique has been learned—the tying of a rug knot, the insertion of a hook into canvas, the treatment of a slit in a tapestry weave—there is no questioning it. Desired results were achieved centuries ago with processes developed to the point where there since has been little need for change because they *work*. Assuredly, less primitive methods of achieving them and new ways of using them have been devised, but the basic concepts remain the same.

Designing the rug, the manner in which those techniques are used, on the other hand, is not a static process; its development cannot reach the stage where a few designs can be isolated as "one of the rug designs." If "this is a good rug design" can be said of one rug design, it can be said of hundreds. It is a creative processing or fruition of ideas which can be expressed in a variety of ways dependent on the penchant and the personality of the person designing. It lends itself to freedom of

v

expression rather than to a set of rules. How to begin to use that freedom, particularly for the more timid beginner, could seem confusing were it not that the techniques themselves necessarily require a degree of discipline and that certain ways of using them suggest possibilities or bases for designs.

Developing an awareness of the passing scene—natural and man-made—is, perhaps, one of the best ways to absorb impressions which eventually will transform themselves into design ideas. To translate these into actual rug designs, one can be guided, if need be, by certain basic design concepts which are not difficult to understand. Instinctively, or with the help of a very elementary knowledge of design principles, one can begin to design rugs. There are all shades of creativity, and all of us have been endowed with one shade or another of it.

Rug designs need not be works of art—they can be simple and uncomplicated and be very successful because they serve the function for which they were made and pleasantly complete the area in which they are placed. Beyond that is an open field which each person can explore in his own time. Familiarity and understanding of any process break down the resistance to exploring it. May the following chapters help stimulate you toward that exploration by giving you an insight into some of the "mysteries" of the craft, and dispelling any fear of exploiting them.

Yes—handmaking a rug *is* for the elect—*you,* the reader of this book.

MARY ALLARD

Contents

RUG MAKING
Techniques and Design

CHAPTER 1

Introduction

RUG DEFINED

A rug for the purposes of this book is a fairly heavy piece of processed "material" designed to cover an area or the entire floor of a room for one of several reasons: furnishing underfoot or atmospheric warmth, creating an air of luxury, softening noises, adding a bit of color to an otherwise dull spot, focusing attention on a specific area, or tying a room or parts of a room into a cohesive unit or units. Depending upon its function, then, a rug and its design can range in type from the very unobtrusive, quiet and soothing to the quite colorful, resplendent and exciting.

The need for the variety of rugs which these various roles create can be satisfied through surprisingly few techniques which, basically, can be grouped into two categories: those that produce pile-surfaced rugs and those that produce flat-surfaced rugs.

Although the rugs themselves need not be confined to one or the other of these categories—they can be fashioned from a combined use of the two—the most logical way to get to know and understand the techniques seems to be to confine them to the two major parts into which this book is divided: **pile rugs** and **flat rugs**. The techniques will be presented as comprehensively as possible and in such a way, it is hoped, that you will be encouraged to use them freely and imaginatively, not necessarily to produce rugs within given categories, but in any way you want or need to express an idea, a mood, or a texture that you wish to capture.

WEAVING

In all but a few cases, making rugs that fall into the pile and flat divisions depends upon the more encompassing process of **weaving.** In a book of this size, it is impossible to cover the broad field of weaving and do justice to its rug-making facets, too. It is therefore assumed that most readers of this book have at least an elementary knowledge of weaving. For those of you who have no such knowledge or who wish to extend your elementary knowledge, it is suggested that you refer to one of the many books on weaving which can be found in most libraries and bookshops. However, since so many of the techniques covered in this book include the use of the plain weave, it might be of help to the nonweaver to give a capsule description of weaving and its simplest form, the plain weave. At the same time, this can serve as a glossary of some of the terms used in this book. It might also be helpful to outline one of the commonly used methods of perform-

FIG. 1. Horizontal loom with warp set in ready to receive filling. (*1*) Cloth beam. (*2*) Breast beam. (*3*) Beater with reed. (*4*) Harnesses with heddles. (*5*) Back beam. (*6*) Warp beam. (*7*) Treadles. (*8*) Warp.

ing the preliminary steps which must be taken before the plain weave, or any weaving, can begin.

WEAVING TERMS DEFINED

Weaving is the interlacing of a set of vertical threads with a set of horizontal threads to form a fabric. The vertical threads collectively are called a **warp,** and singly are called **ends,** or warp ends. The horizontal threads collectively are called **filling,** or weft, and singly are called **picks,** or filling picks. The warp is made up of a fixed number of ends which are stretched side by side onto a framelike device called a **loom;** the warp is kept in place by being rolled onto a **warp beam** at one end and a **cloth beam** at

the other end of the loom. The warp beam holds the unwoven warp, the cloth beam will eventually hold the woven fabric. To facilitate the interlacing of the filling with the warp, the filling yarn is usually rolled onto a spool or **bobbin** which in turn is placed into a boat-shaped receptacle called a **shuttle.** So that it will not be necessary for the filling to pick its way laboriously in a mending fashion across the width of the warp, most looms are equipped with some sort of "shedding motion" which allows specific sets of warp ends to be raised or lowered while others remain in place. Most looms have at least two **harnesses** which make this shedding motion possible; these are frames which hold a series of parallel wires, with eyes in the middle, called **heddles.** Each

2

of the warp ends is separately **drawn,** or threaded, into the eye of one of the heddles in one of the harnesses. The raising of a particular harness by means of a **treadle** necessarily raises all of the warp ends which have been drawn into the heddles within that harness, while all other ends remain below. This creates a space between the ends which are up and those which are down, making it possible to shoot the shuttle from one side of the warp to the other with one motion. This space is called a **shed.** When all ends are at rest, a shed is referred to as **closed;** when some ends are up and others down, the shed is referred to as **open.**

The sequence of harnesses in which the ends have been drawn, and the order in which the harnesses are raised and lowered to form sheds for the picks of filling to pass through, create certain patterns called **weaves.** When the filling in the first row, or pick, goes over all odd warp ends, and under all even warp ends, and in the second pick under all odd warp ends, and over all even warp ends, the weave is called a **plain weave.** Alternately drawing one end into the first harness and the next into the second harness of a 2-harness loom, and continuing so until all ends are drawn in, will place all odd ends into the first harness and all even ends into the second harness. Raising harness 1 will, therefore, open up the shed of the first pick of the plain weave, and raising harness 2 will open up the shed of the second pick of the plain weave. Continuation of the process of alternately raising harness 1 and harness 2 will result in a plain weave fabric. In the making of most rugs, the plain weave is interrupted at intervals for the insertion of pile yarn or other applied surface, but continues as a sort of secondary but very essential theme to build up a foundation for the rug.

FIG. 2. Open shed.

3

Each pick inserted into a fabric must be beaten into place either with a **hand beater,** a comblike device, or, as is more often the case, with a **beater** built into and stretching all the way across the loom, into which the comblike device called a **reed** has been inserted. The "comb" or reed, in this case, stretches across the weaving width of the loom, and is made up of a series of metal strips held in place by a lower and upper rib. The spaces between the strips are called **dents** into which the warp ends (after having been drawn into the harnesses) are **sleyed,** or threaded. Thus the warp is kept in place and stretched throughout the weaving to establish the density and width of the woven fabric. Reeds are interchangeable; some have many dents, and others have few dents per inch. The many-dents-per-inch reeds are used for fine fabrics, the few-dents-per-inch ones for coarser fabrics; an 8-dent, or 6-dent reed mentioned so often later, refers to one with 8 dents per inch, or 6 dents per inch. An 8-ends-per-inch warp would be sleyed one end in each dent of an 8-dent reed; a 6-ends-per-inch warp would be sleyed one end in each dent of a 6-dent reed. It is possible and often practical or necessary to sley more than one end per dent, or to leave some dents without ends. One pull of the loom beater will beat the pick in place, whereas several of the hand beater are necessary before it has beaten the pick the whole width of the loom.

PRELIMINARY STEPS TO WEAVING

Since the warp is a premeasured and fixed unit around which the weaving revolves, no part of the weaving process can begin before it is made up. The first step toward making the warp is planning the rug, at least to the point where it is known what technique will be used and what the width and the length of the rug will be, because those are the facts that determine the kind of yarn which will make up the warp, the number of ends per inch, the total number of ends in the warp, and the length of the warp. In certain types of rugs, the surface design must also be decided upon because it too can be a determining factor in the makeup of the warp.

For clarity's sake, let us assume that the warp being set up is to be used for one of the rugs described in this book using the plain weave as its basic structure. This includes most of the pile rugs, the tapestry rug, and the soumak. Let the project be a rug 5 feet long, and let it be made the full width of the capacity of a 24-inch loom, or 2 feet wide.

The warp yarn will be 10-ply cotton cord set at 8 ends per inch. Since the width of the rug is to be 24 inches, the total number of ends in the warp will be 8 x 24, or 192 ends.

The length of the warp must be the length of the rug—5 feet—plus a certain number of inches that must remain unwoven. Some of this is used for tying onto the front and sometimes the back of the loom, some for the portion at the beginning of the warp which must be used for stabilizing it before the weaving of the actual rug can begin, and some for that portion at the end of the warp which is prevented by the harnesses from coming far enough in front of the beater to be woven. One yard, or 3 feet, is in most cases more than adequate for this waste. In addition to this, an extra length must be allowed for "take-up" caused by the fact that the warp usually cannot weave in a perfectly straight manner, but must take a sinuous course over and under the picks of filling. In some weaves like the tapestry in which the filling completely covers the warp—and some of the pile rugs if the filling is treated in the tapestry manner—the take-up is slight because most of the waviness occurs in the filling; in certain other types of weaves, the take-up can be quite high. In this case it is low and 20 per cent of the 5-foot length of the rug—1 foot—should be a sufficient amount to allow. It is always better to end up with a little too much than not quite enough warp! Adding together the length of the rug, waste, and take-up—5 plus 3 plus 1—gives a total warp length of 9 feet, or 3 yards.

The length of the warp, 3 yards (which is synonymous with the length of each end), multiplied by the number of ends in the warp, 192, tells us that 576 yards will be needed for the entire warp. Since there are about 600 yards to the pound of 10-ply cotton cord, 1 pound of yarn would be needed for a rug such as this one.

MAKING UP THE WARP

The device used in this example for making up the warp is called a **warping frame** which acts as a unit of measurement for each warp end. In most frames, the horizontal space between pegs is 1 yard. Since the warp yarn is carried around the pegs and stretched from one side of the frame to the other, one stretch across the frame is normally 1 yard of warp.

1. Tie the cotton cord warp yarn (which usually comes on cones) to a peg the length of the warp away—in this case 3 yards—from the upper right hand peg. Holding the yarn under even and firm tension, but not too tight or it will pull the pegs in, carry it around the peg horizontally across and slightly above the beginning peg. Continue crossing from side to side until the upper crosspiece is reached. Bring yarn over first peg. It is at this point that the **cross**, or lease, which keeps each end in its proper sequence, begins. It is important that this cross be maintained because without it the warp would be very difficult to set into the loom. Bring yarn over the middle peg of the crosspiece and under the last one. This completes the first warp end. To begin

the second warp end, finish cross by going around and over the last peg at top of crosspiece and under the middle one. One repeat of the cross is now completed. Continue winding second warp end by going over the next peg on upper crosspiece and retracing the path of the first end exactly. Retrace these first two ends until the warp is completed, and finish by cutting off the warp yarn from its source and tying the end to the beginning peg. The warp does not need to be made all in one section—if it is fat, it is easier to make it in two or more sections.

2. Secure the cross in place by tying each of its four sides loosely with cord.

3. It is not necessary, but it is helpful in holding the warp in place, to wind a piece of cord tightly twice around every yard or two of the warp. This cord should be bowknotted in place so that it can be pulled apart easily when the warp is being wound onto the warp beam.

4. The warp is taken off the frame gradually by chaining. Face the direction in which the warp is going and with the left hand, palm up, grasp warp firmly a few inches above the beginning peg; cut yarn away from, or slip it off, the first peg. Grasp the warp with the right hand, palm up, at a point a few inches above the left hand. Bring left hand forward, twist right hand until palm is down to form a loop with the warp. Holding the loop with left hand, put right hand through loop, pick up entire warp, and pull it through to form another loop. Continue to chain by forming new loops until about a foot of warp is left. Slip the rest of the warp off the upper crosspiece. Change the position of your body during chaining to accommodate change in direction of the warp as it stretches from side to side.

5

FIG. 3. The first 2 ends of a warp, showing the cross being formed.

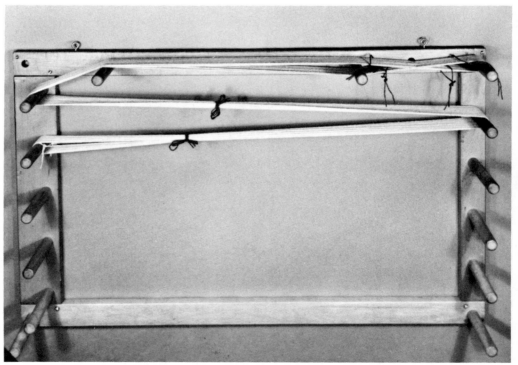

FIG. 4. The completed warp with the 4 sides of the cross tied in place, and with ties placed tightly around the whole warp every yard to hold the warp together at intervals.

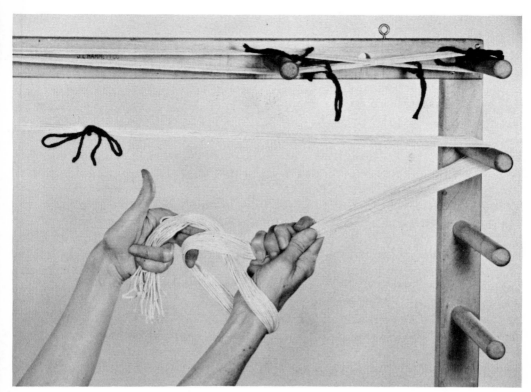

FIG. 5. Removing the warp from the frame—the first loop in the chain.

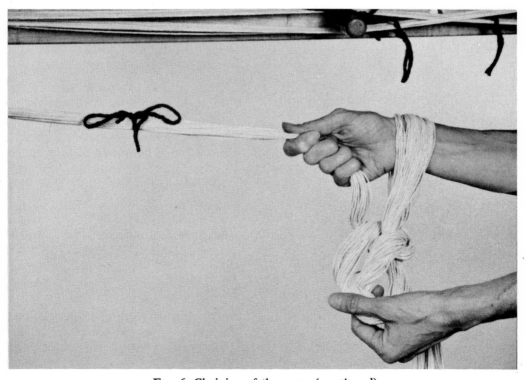

FIG. 6. Chaining of the warp (*continued*).

7

SETTING THE WARP INTO THE LOOM

Remove the beater—and the harnesses if they are going to interfere with winding the warp to its full width onto the warp beam—or else push the heddles away from the middle to the sides of the harnesses. With this method, two **lease sticks** and a spreader called a **raddle** will be needed. The lease sticks will eventually replace the cords which have been holding the cross, or lease, in place. The raddle is used to spread the warp to full width while winding it onto the warp beam. It can be made quite easily by hammering all but an inch or so of round-headed nails spaced an inch apart into and all the way across a smooth stick about $1\frac{1}{2}''$ x $1''$ in girth, and at least the loom-width long. The manufactured raddles have grooved tops which fit onto the nails after the warp has been spread to prevent the ends from slipping out of place when the warp is being wound, but a piece of cord wrapped below the head of each nail will work just as well.

1. Bring stick attached to warp beam over the back beam and insert it into the looped section of the cross at the end of the warp. Place the rest of the warp still chained through to the front of the loom and over the breast beam. So that the raddle and lease sticks will have a support on which to rest, insert on each side of the loom a stick long enough to stretch over the back and breast beams, or tie a heavy cord to the front and back beams on each side of the loom. Insert one lease stick in each section of the cross, or lease, and tie them together on either side so that the warp will not slip out. Cut off the strings that tied the cross together. Place the raddle in front of the lease sticks and under the warp. Spread and center the warp with the aid of the raddle by inserting each inch of warp (8 ends in this case) between the inch spaces in the raddle. This should be done gently so that the ends are not

disturbed from their relative position in the warp.

2. The winding is usually done by two persons, one holding the warp evenly and under firm tension from in front of the breast beam while the other rolls it onto the warp beam and inserts sheets of heavy paper, extending beyond the warp on either side, between the layers of warp until the warp is rolled to about a foot in front of the harnesses. The unchaining and releasing of the tie cords is done gradually with the winding of the warp. The lease sticks and raddle should be kept close to the harnesses by pushing them or tying them in place. Winding can be done by one person if the rolling of about a foot or so of warp is alternated with pulling the warp firmly to tension the portion of it which has already been rolled on. The warp should not be combed—a firm shake or pull now and then will help to stabilize the warp if necessary. When winding is completed, remove the raddle and pull the lease sticks forward so that the ends can be seen from the space between the lease sticks and picked up readily in their proper sequence.

3. Draw the ends into the harnesses from the front of the loom. It is usually more comfortable to remove the breast beam so that you can get closer to the work. Insert a reed hook into the eye of the first heddle at the left of the first harness (the one closest to you). Pick up the first end from the left of the warp, and pull it with the reed hook through the heddle; push it away to the left. Insert the reed hook into the eye of the first heddle at the left of the second harness, pick up the second or next end and pull it through. Then push it away to the left. This is one repeat of what is termed a straight draw, on a 2-harness loom for a plain weave. Repeat this until all ends have been drawn in. In a single repeat of

8

the same draw in a 4-harness loom, the ends would be inserted in a harness sequence of 1, 2, 3, 4.

4. Lay the reed horizontally, resting it on the cross sticks or ties. Center the warp into the reed. Starting from center of the reed and center of the warp, sley the ends 1 to a dent in an 8-dent reed, working outward toward the left and right until all ends have been sleyed. Secure the warp into the reed by slip-knotting small bunches of warp so that the ends won't fall out at this, the point where the reed is placed into the beater.

5. Pull the stick attached to the cloth beam over the breast beam and attach the warp to it in small bunches of about an inch. Tighten the ends evenly and separate each bunch in half; bring both over and under the stick, with the left hand half coming around to the left and the right hand half around to the right of the entire bunch. Tie together with a single knot. Less loosening will occur if the order of tying is one bunch at either of the extreme edges, one in the center, alternating with a few bunches first to the right and then to the left of center, until complete warp is tied. Tighten the single knots in the same order and tie each with a double knot. Try out the tension by passing the hand lightly across the warp in back of the reed. Readjust by pulling out and retying bunches not under proper tension.

6. Tighten the warp to weaving tension. Test with plain weave treadling to see that no errors have been made in drawing-in and sleying and, if so, remove the lease sticks. Stabilize the warp by weaving a few picks at a time and beating hard, and repeating until the warp is evenly spaced. Weaving of the rug can now begin.

EQUIPMENT FOR WOVEN RUGS

Since, as already stated, woven rugs are but one of the products of the process of weaving itself, rug-weaving equipment is the same as that for any other form of weaving. Some people can and want to get along with the barest of equipment and others prefer to work with more conveniences. It is possible to make rugs with practically no equipment—some extremely beautiful ones have been woven on looms fashioned of just two sticks—but it does make life easier and it is not an extravagance to have equipment with some time- and labor-saving devices.

The loom need not have been built especially to make rugs, but it should be a sturdy enough floor loom to withstand the heavy beating a rug requires. Although for some types of rugs, as mentioned further along in the text, it is possible to use vertical looms, on the whole it will be found that, even for those rugs, the horizontal loom with harnesses is easier and more comfortable for most people to use.

Looms come, or can be made, in various weaving widths that automatically establish the maximum width of any rug or fabric to be made on them. Disregarding any shrinkage that might occur in the width after a rug has been taken off the loom, a 36-inch- or 40-inch-wide loom will weave no wider than a 36- or 40-inch-wide rug, respectively. Narrower rugs than maximum loom width can, of course, be woven. It is sometimes possible to sew strips together to form wider rugs. In such a case, unless it is a random-type flat rug, the strips should be measured often and woven carefully as the strips progress, so that matching will not become a problem when sewing them together with strong carpet thread.

Other equipment normally used for weaving, such as warping reel or frame, bobbin winder, spool rack, swift or skein winder, and shuttles, though not all essential, will be found useful and convenient.

Equipment necessary or useful to the making of rugs which is not typically used for other types of weaving is discussed under the sections covering those particular types of rugs.

FIG. 7. The warp centered and spaced at the back of the loom, ready to be rolled onto the warp beam. Stick attached to warp beam and one lease stick inserted into end loop of cross; other lease stick inserted into second part of cross; warp spaced and centered into raddle or spreader, secured within its inch spaces by string wrapped around nails.

FIG. 8. Ends being drawn into the heddles from the front of the loom.

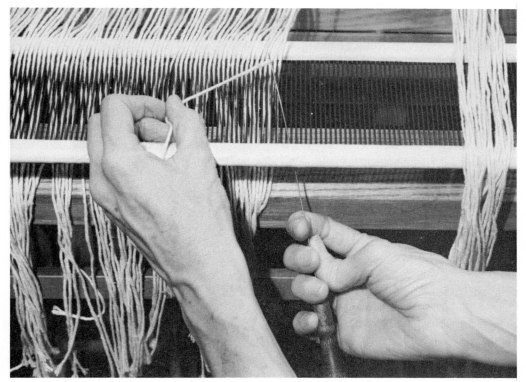

FIG. 9. Ends being sleyed into the reed from the front of the loom.

FIG. 10. The warp being tied in bunches to the stick attached to the cloth beam.

YARNS OR MATERIALS

Since the warp and some of the filling in most rugs discussed in this book do not show, good grades of cotton cord, as suggested in the sections covering the various techniques, are quite satisfactory.

For pile and other yarns that are visible on the surface of the rug, wool is the near-ideal fiber of the many yarns available because it has, to a great degree, all of the qualities one usually looks for in a rug. It is strong and durable, it has body and resilience, it takes and holds dye beautifully, it resists dirt, and it can be dry cleaned. In addition to all these virtues, it has a richness that can range from the soft and lustrous to the rugged and energetic, depending upon how loosely or tightly the strands have been twisted or plied together. Its properties are seldom incompatible with other important factors which should not be overlooked when making the final choice of yarn for a rug: the use to which the rug is to be put, the technique to be used, and the time it will take to make it. The only one of these in which it falls short, admittedly not very often, is "the use to which the rug is to be put." Wool would definitely be impractical, for instance, for rugs that would need to be laundered rather than dry cleaned, such as most bathroom rugs and perhaps those for small children's rooms. It is a "natural" for any of the techniques covered in this book, and is particularly suitable for use in those rugs whose techniques are time-consuming, such as the knotted pile rug, because it wears long and well. It is always advisable to use materials of good quality when making anything by hand, and particularly so in cases where the technique takes a long time—it is practical to use a quality of yarn commensurate with the time required to make the rug. It would be a pity to spend days, sometimes weeks, making a beautiful rug only to have it wear out in a short while. However, this should not discourage anyone from having the pleasure of using a time-consuming technique, if one is willing or is forced to use materials of lesser quality for any of a number of valid reasons, such as during the learning process, when cost of materials is a factor, or when weaving for therapeutic purposes.

The fact that wool has so many qualitative properties does not necessarily make it the only fiber worthy of use in making rugs. There are other yarns or materials, some more readily available than others— linen, ramie, handspun wool or cotton rovings, some synthetics, jute, sisal, strips of cloth or felt—each with its own individual character and with properties in one degree or another which make it suitable for particular rugs. The wearing quality of a yarn will depend on the foot traffic it will have to bear as well as the technique which will be used. A rug for an area where little activity goes on and only soft-soled shoes are worn does not have to be made with as durable a yarn as a rug for a highly trafficked area subject to wear and abrasion from street shoes. A fiber too weak for one technique will be stronger with another. For instance, cotton or wool roving, usually a fairly bulky but single-plied and loosely twisted yarn, would soon wear out if used for a cut-pile rug where the tufts of yarn are vulnerable because fully exposed on the surface, whereas its life expectancy would increase considerably if used in a flat weave where it is closely interlaced with strong warp yarn.

Resilience in a fiber also lessens in importance when a flat rather than a pile technique is used; the yarn is already held down in a flat weave so that it does not have as far to spring back after being stepped on as it does in a pile rug. Yet even in a pile rug, particularly looped pile, the brittle quality of a durable fiber such as linen sometimes provides a texture that would best fit in with the mood of the area or room where it is to be placed, even if it is less resilient and more crushable than wool. The tone of a room—its formality or informality; its furnishings; its use; the user's preference—all play a part in the type of fiber one might use.

Climatic conditions also have a lot to do with choice of yarn; the coolness of linen or cotton can have a refreshing effect in warmer climates or seasons. Good grades of both are durable and easy to take care of because normally washable. The color range is good and usually fast. Ramie is a very durable and attractive fiber, cool in aspect but, unfortunately, not easily obtainable. Sisal and jute are also comfortable warm-climate fibers. Good grades of both are fairly durable but not especially colorfast; they are attractive in their natural or bleached states, however, if colorfastness is an important consideration. Sisal is a stiff fiber that is not overly pliant so that it usually cannot be woven very firmly on most handlooms, and therefore tends to fall apart more readily. It can be used with other fibers in such ways

that this tendency will be lessened considerably.

Fibers do not have to be used by themselves. Each has a character attractive unto itself, but its textural qualities are often more effective and even more pronounced when used as highlights in contrast to other fibers.

The element of experimentation should not be overlooked. The only way to know how some yarns behave is to try them out. Particularly is this true of synthetic yarns available to handweavers. Their content so often varies that it is impossible to appraise them without at least seeing and feeling them.

It is possible to obtain some rug yarns in yarn shops or department stores, but a wider variety is obtainable and it is usually more economical to buy them from distributors who regularly service handweavers. They are sold by the pound or portions of a pound from samples that are available at no cost or at a nominal fee.

FIG. 11. Double prayer rug, Persian, end of 17th century. Sehna knot. (Courtesy of The Metropolitan Museum of Art, The James F. Ballard Collection, Gift of James F. Ballard, 1922.)

14

PILE RUGS

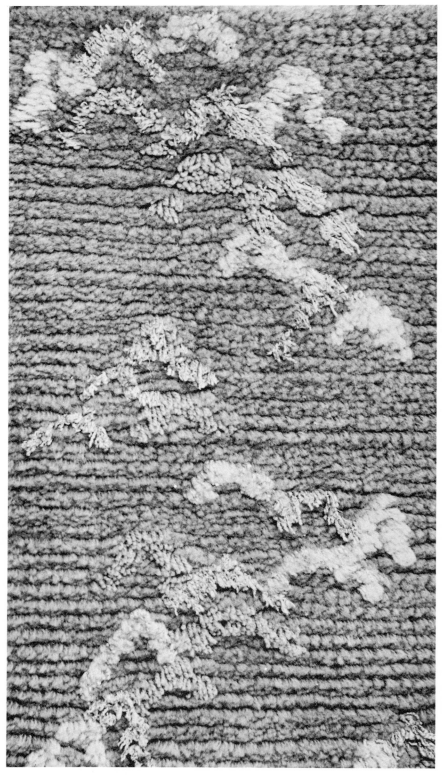

FIG. 12. Wool with 2 pile heights, textured rayon for lustrous accent.
Ghiordes knot.

CHAPTER 2

Historical Notes

Many centuries ago someone conceived the idea of extending looped or cut bits of yarn beyond and more or less perpendicular to a piece of fabric. This gave to what would otherwise have been a flat fabric a shaggy, furry, or velvety appearance which we call **pile.** The bits of yarn forming the pile were sometimes merely inserted into the fabric while it was being woven, and sometimes secured to the warp by means of knots at intervals between the weaving of the fabric.

The earliest fragments so far found of both the unknotted and knotted types— usually only patterned with pile, and occasionally with the pattern on both sides of the fabric—have been from Egypt and made of linen. Among what are probably some of the earliest known remnants of the pile technique are towels from Egyptian tombs of the XI Dynasty (about 2000 B.C.). The pile in those towels is unknotted and was devised by pulling up the filling at regular intervals into loops extending beyond the plain-weave foundation of the fabric.

Other pile fabrics of this and later eras, made in the same manner as the towels, were used in clothing with the pile to be worn close to the body for warmth. Needless to say, our Turkish towels can easily find an ancestor in this pile fabric.

But we are concerned with rugs. What are known as Alpujarras from Spain and many other rugs were and are still made of the same pile construction. The hooked rug is undoubtedly an outgrowth of this type of construction. It is believed by many historians that early in the Christian era and probably before, this type of loop (sometimes cut) was also at times pushed into rather than woven into a fabric.

The fact that the Egyptians could use pile freely for such varied purposes as towels and wearing apparel shows that, even at such an early date, they were very much at home with the craft—that they had achieved a degree of skill and flexibility which permitted them to adapt the pile technique to fabrics with various uses, and in various ways. If no floor coverings were then being made with the technique, it could certainly not be because they lacked the imagination to do so—it must have been because floor coverings had not come into their own in the social scheme of things.

Fragments dated some 500 or so years later than the towels indicate that development of the technique had not stood still. By then, if such had not happened sooner, the pile was being knotted. One of those remnants housed at the New York Metropolitan Museum has quite a dense cut pile about 3 inches long done in a diamond-shaped pattern, achieved by a

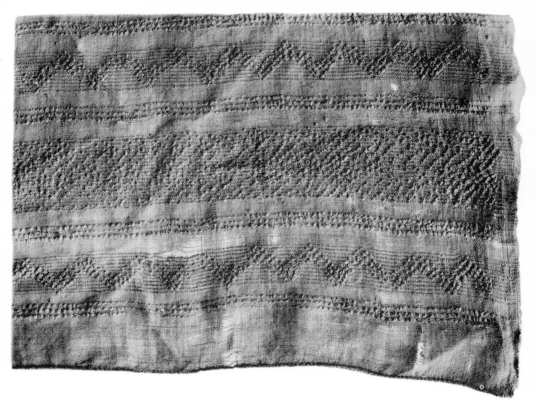

FIG. 13. Assasif, Tomb 813. Fragment of linen towel with looped pile. XI Dynasty. (Photograph by Egyptian Expedition. Courtesy of The Metropolitan Museum of Art.)

FIG. 14. Looped pile rug. Ana Segura, artist. Made in Las Alpujarras, Granada province, Spain, 1766. (Courtesy of The Hispanic Society of America.)

knot attached to a single warp end. If this and others like it were not used as floor coverings, again it must have been because of social custom. While at present it looks much like shredded wheat, the material could have had quite a deeply luxuriant feel to the bare feet when it was soft and new some 3500 years ago.

Our present-day parallel of this technique is found in most knotted rugs from Spain. In some quarters, this same knot is known as the "Spanish" knot because the Spaniards have used it consistently for centuries in the majority of their knotted rugs.

A fabric with the same knotted pile, but made with the barbs of ostrich feathers, may even predate the Egyptian linen-piled ones just described. These were thought to have been used as rugs. Whatever the sequence of dates, and whatever their use, it is another tribute to the versatility and skill of the ancient Egyptian who could visualize and make use of different materials to develop new types of fabric. This was excavated in Kerma but attributed to Egyptian craftsmen living there during the occupation of Nubia by the Egyptians.

This is intended to indicate something of what is presently known about the variously formed techniques which later permitted great works of art to come into being, and which still persist in our day, rather than to extol the Egyptian as the originator of the pile. While there is no denying the fact that the Egyptians' use of the pile technique had been very well developed at a very early period and that it took on different forms, there is no conclusive evidence that their influence was responsible for the use of the technique in other parts of the Eastern world. It could well have developed simultaneously in Asian areas without outside influences. While archaeological evidence proves the age-old existence of such techniques in Egypt, there are too many gaps between finds in other areas to prove conclusively single or multiple origin, or

FIG. 15. Back and front of a linen pile fragment, done with a single warp knot. From Thebes. Egyptian XVII–XVIII Dynasty. (Courtesy of The Metropolitan Museum of Art, Museum Excavations, 1915–1916.)

to enable us to follow its early stage-by-stage development. Nor can it be determined at what point in that development the technique emerged into floor-covering form.

Although no earlier pile fabrics seem to have been found in the Asian area, the fragment, undeniably a carpet, excavated from the Altai Mountains of Central Asia and dated at 500 B.C., shows such a skillful use of the pile technique that it must have had several centuries of anterior development. This, unlike the Egyptian pile fabrics, which were all of natural-color linen and which resorted to partial pile for design, was an all-pile rug made of various colors of wool in a figured design. It was made with a two-warp rather than a single-warp knot. Whether or not this

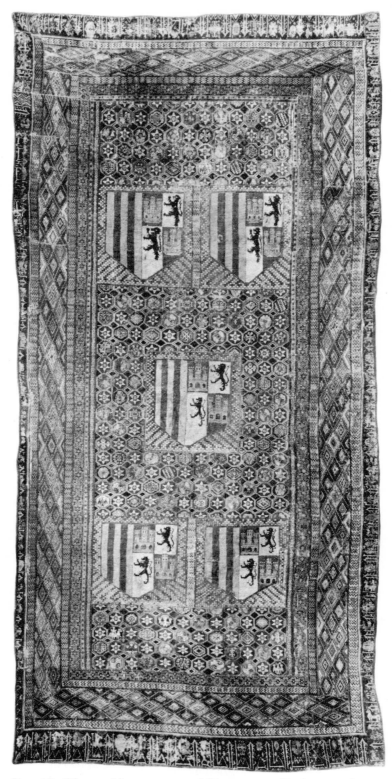

Fig. 16. Hispano-Moresque rug, 15th century. Single warp knot.
(Courtesy of The Hispanic Society of America.)

20

FIG. 17. Detail of the Hispano-Moresque rug shown in Fig. 16. (Courtesy of The Hispanic Society of America.)

FIG. 18. Fragment of an Egyptian wool rug, Coptic, ca. A.D. 400, found at Antinoe, Egypt. Sehna knot achieved through looping. (Courtesy of The Metropolitan Museum of Art, Rogers Fund, 1931.)

was an import from somewhere else in the East is unknown—but, somewhere in the Eastern world, and long before the Christian era, knotted pile wool carpets of a well-developed kind were being made.

A Coptic rug fragment dated at about A.D. 400 is a good example of another method of knotting. This, too, was so skillfully treated that such a stage could not have been reached without long previous development.

By the sixteenth century, probably the richest rugs ever known were being produced in Turkey and Persia, the Turkish ones with the same knot as that of the Altai Mountain fragment, and the Persian ones with a variation of the Coptic rug

of Fig. 18. These became known as "Ghiordes" and "Sehna" knots probably because exquisite examples of the Oriental rug art were being woven with those respective knots in the towns of Ghiordes, Turkey, and Sehna, Persia. Since "Ghiordes" and "Sehna" became synonymous with the acme of perfection in rugs, could enterprising rug traders have seen the advertising power in the adoption of the names for all rugs made with those knots?

The spread of these age-old techniques to the Western world can be traced from the early centuries of our era. Though eventually, as in the Eastern countries, they too began to reflect the ideas and

1. Rug in 2 heights of cut and looped pile, done with Ghiordes and reversed Ghiordes knot.

2. Pile and tapestry weave rug. Cut pile and braid made with Ghiordes knot.

3. Experimental "soumak" rug.

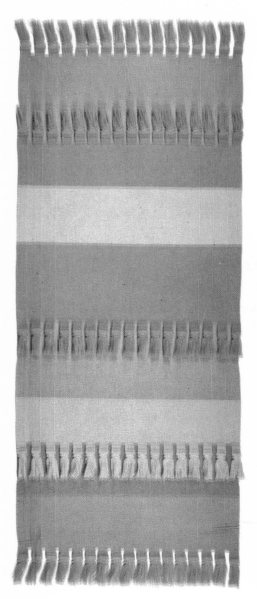

4. Fringed tapestry weave rug. Tabs done on extra warp ends.

5. Contemporary double cloth rug.

FIG. 19. Turkish pile rug, late 16th–17th century. Ghiordes knot. (Courtesy of The Metropolitan Museum of Art, The James F. Ballard Collection, Gift of James F. Ballard, 1922.)

FIG. 20. French 17th-century wool rug, Savonnerie. Ghiordes knot. (Courtesy of The Metropolitan Museum of Art, Gift of Mrs. Robert Armstrong, 1958.)

fashions of the countries of adoption, thus taking on characteristics of their own, they still were made with the same basic construction, and are to the present day. The old Savonneries and the present-day Aubussons of France, the Scandinavian flossas and ryas, some presently made Iranian and Turkish and many others including some made in this country, are fashioned with the knot of the Altai Mountain fragment; the Chinese and some of the Iranian and Turkish people still use the Sehna knot.

FIG. 21. Contemporary Ghiordes knotted ramie rug, made in Taiwan. (Taiwanese photograph by permission of *Handweaver and Craftsman* magazine.)

CHAPTER 3

The Woven Pile Rug with Knots

A woven knotted pile rug is made up basically of one or more rows of plain weave alternating with one row of pile, repeated over and over again until the rug is finished. Monotonous? Not unless one thinks purely in terms of the mechanics of the making of the rug without considering the satisfaction derived from seeing the pile build up, or the creative aspect of manipulating the process to express an idea.

The pile is made up of strands of yarn, not interlaced with but attached to the warp by means of knots, several of which are required to make one row of pile, each one representing a minute portion of the rug and its design. They are not knots as we are used to thinking of them—the yarn is wrapped around the warp rather than tied to it. However, when the warp and filling that form the foundation of the rug are properly woven together to hold the knots in place, the pile is really knotted because it cannot be pulled out without really trying.

Since the pile cannot be separated from the knot, the term **knot** when used in this book means not only the part of the pile yarn wrapped around the warp ends but every part of it, including the tufts of it which stand up more or less perpendicularly to form the pile.

Because its perpendicular position frees the knot from the foundation fabric that holds the pile together, each knot becomes a separate unit which can have its own color, its own texture, its own pile height. This means that the surface design can change at any point where there is a knot. Since the space taken up by each knot is small, the closeness of the points at which the lines of the surface design can potentially move makes the knotted pile a very flexible medium for a variously shaped motif type of design, usually more characteristic of a print rather than a woven fabric which must depend upon combinations of warp and filling arrangement for its design structure.

Before going any farther, let us look at the woven knotted pile rug in skeletal form and then build up its various aspects with more detailed information. Its progress step by step is as follows:

1. The rug is planned.
2. The warp is made up, set into the loom for plain weave, and stabilized with preliminary weaving.
3. The hem is woven in, later to be turned under or left to show as part of the design.
4. Yarn for wrapping edges is inserted at both sides of the warp.
5. One row of knots is tied with pile yarn onto the warp according to de-

FIG. 22. Ghiordes knotted wool rug sample with 2 heights of pile.

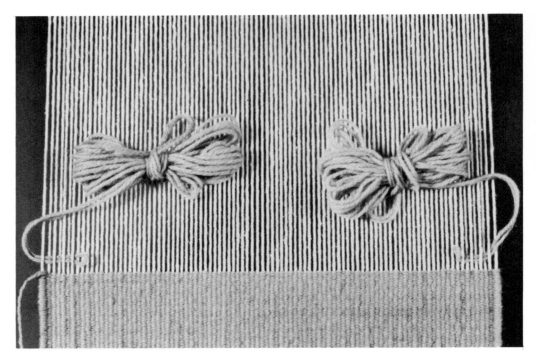

FIG. 23. The hem is woven in and yarn for wrapping the edges of the rug inserted.

FIG. 24. The first row of pile is made, leaving the first and the last ends free of knots.

FIG. 25. Filling is inserted to hold the pile in place and the edge wrapped at the insertion point of each pick. The last inserted pick is shown before it is beaten into the rug.

sign, leaving the first and last warp ends free of knots.

6. Picks of plain-weave filling are inserted in order to hold the knots in place, and the edge at insertion side of each pick is wrapped with edge-wrapping yarn.

7. Steps 5 and 6 are repeated until rug is finished, ending with a pile row.

8. Edge-wrapping yarn is tucked into the warp and cut off.

9. The hem is woven, just as in Step 3.

10. The rug is cut off the loom and finished at the ends with fringe, or turned-under hems.

THE KNOTS

The three basic knots which are used to build up pile are made as follows:

The Ghiordes

This knot is usually made from left to right and requires at least 2 warp ends per knot. It is made while the shed is closed by bringing the pile yarn from the right of, and under and over, the left-hand warp end; then over and under the right-hand warp end. The knots should come as close as possible to the last pick of weaving by pulling the pile ends toward the weaving as the knot is being tied. From the illustration—and from trial on the loom—it can be noted that the ends of yarn which form the pile come under the loop of the knot and fall toward the beginning of the rug. There is no reason why this cannot be made from right to left if one finds it easier to do so, in which case the instructions would apply in reverse.

29

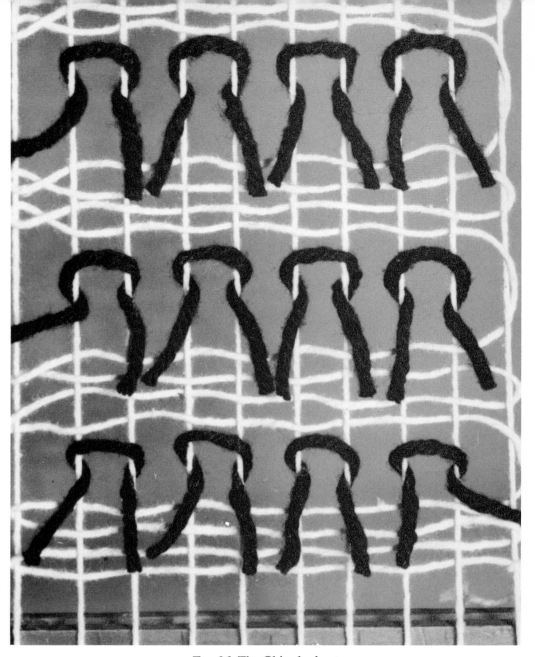

FIG. 26. The Ghiordes knot.

The Sehna

LEFT-HAND. It seems easier when working from left to right to use what is termed the "left-hand" Sehna which encircles only the left warp end of the pair of warp ends used to make the knot. It is made while the shed is closed by inserting the pile yarn from the right of, and under and over, the left-hand end; then coming to the surface from under the right-hand end of the two warp ends used to com-

plete the knot. The pile ends of the knot are pulled close to the last pick of weaving as knot is being tied to bring the knot in place. The pile has a tendency to fall toward the right.

RIGHT-HAND. The "right-hand" Sehna, called so because the pile encircles only the right end of the pair of warp ends used to make the knot, seems to work more fluidly when tied from right to left. It is made while the shed is closed by in-

30

FIG. 27. Persian Garden Carpet, 1700–1750. Wool with Ghiordes knot. (Courtesy of The Metropolitan Museum of Art, The James F. Ballard Collection, Gift of James F. Ballard, 1922.)

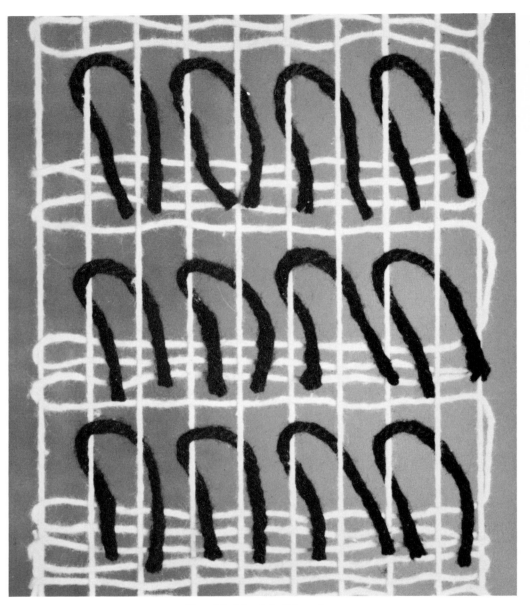

FIG. 28. The left Sehna knot.

serting the pile yarn from the left of, and under and over the right-hand warp end, then coming to the surface from under the left-hand end of the two warp ends used to complete the knot. The pile ends of the knot are pulled close to the last pick of weaving as the knot is being tied. The pile has a tendency to fall toward the left.

The early Persian rugs made with this knot sometimes alternated one row left Sehna, the other row right Sehna. This might have been so only for ease of workmanship; but, since they were well aware of the effect of very fine nuances and subtleties, it could also have been done to take advantage of the play of light, if only slight, that would result from the yarn's tendency to fall first in one direction and then in the other.

Except when the direction of the pile is important in a design, there seems to be no particular advantage of one over

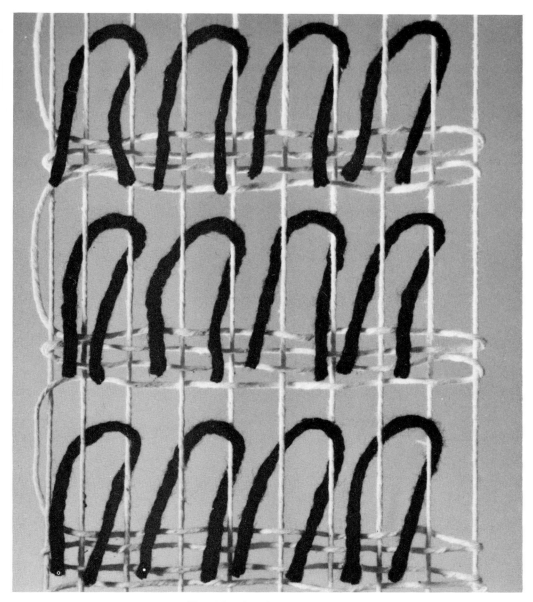

FIG. 29. The right Sehna knot.

the other in these types of knots. More Sehnas can be tied to the inch because the pile is evenly distributed between each warp end rather than between every two warp ends as in the Ghiordes; but that need not concern the contemporary weaver; it is doubtful that he will ever want to make a rug with so many knots per square inch. It has been said that the Ghiordes is an easier knot to tie—but surely that is purely personal—neither knot is difficult to make. Most people in this part of the world use the Ghiordes, the reason probably being that it was the only knot they were taught to make—they might not have known its name or that any other existed.

Single-Warp

This is a knot in which the pile yarn is twisted around a single warp end rather than two. It is made by bringing a length

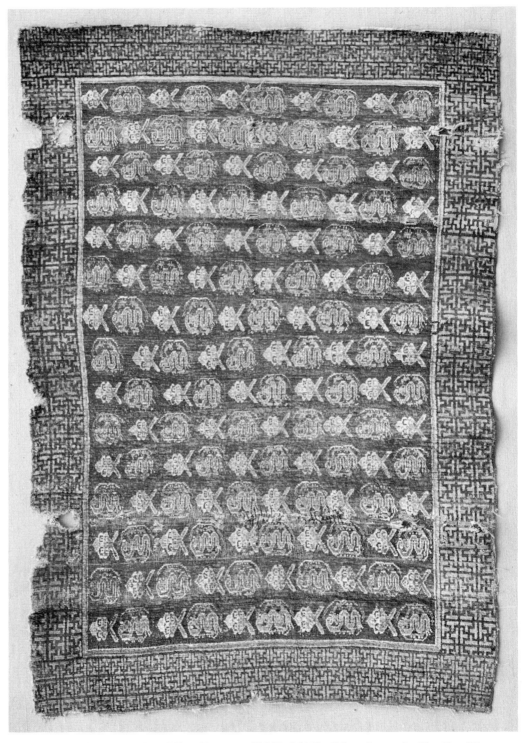

Fig. 30. Chinese rug, late Ming Dynasty (1368–1644). Sehna-knotted silk pile. (Courtesy of The Metropolitan Museum of Art, Rogers Fund, 1908.)

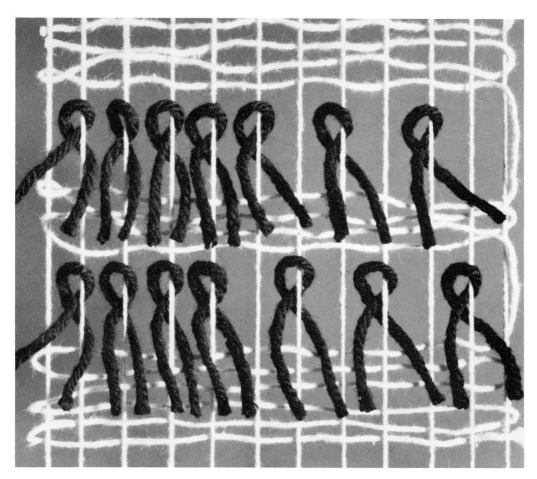

F. 31. The single warp knot. Knots at left tied on every warp end, knots at right tied in alternate rows on alternate warp ends, as they are in most Spanish rugs.

of pile yarn under, over, and under a single warp end so that tufts of pile extend from either side of that warp end. This knot, like all others, should be pulled close to the last filling pick as the knot is being made. It too should be made with a closed shed, unless you wish to use it as the Spaniards do by tying knots in one row of pile onto the odd warp ends only, and in the next row onto the even warp ends only. In that case, it would be easier to use an open shed and tie knots to odd ends while the odd ends are raised, and to even ends while the even ends are raised.

Actually, you may be tempted to use this knot only when there are fine details to be worked into a small area, in a rug which otherwise is not detailed enough to warrant a warp that is finely spaced overall. Using one warp end per knot would make it possible to have twice as many knots as using two warp ends per knot, thus giving the opportunity for twice the amount of change or detail within a given space.

EFFECTS WITH PILE

Although shown as such in the preceding photos for purposes of clearer illustration, each separate knot does not have to be cut, nor does each have to be made with a single strand of yarn. It is a very flexible medium which can be used in a variety of ways to produce an aston-

35

FIG. 32. Spanish rug, 17th–early 18th century. Made at
Cuenca. Single warp knot. (Courtesy of The Hispanic Society of America.)

FIG. 33. Detail of the Spanish rug shown in Fig. 32.

ishing number of effects. The following are but a few of the many ways in which the knot can be treated to translate the shapes of your design into rug form:

1. Yarns can vary in texture, luster, thickness, twist, color—in the same or in separate knots.
2. Pile can be of uniform height—all low and velvety; all high and shaggy.
3. Pile can be of varied heights.
4. Pile can be all cut, all looped, or in combinations of the two.
5. Pile can be combined with flat weaves.
6. Pile can vary in thickness or density from one area of a rug to another.
7. Very low areas of pile can be placed close to very high areas of pile for delineation of shapes.

FIG. 34. Detail of the back of the Spanish rug shown in Fig. 32, showing the single warp knot in alternate rows on alternate warp ends.

37

FIG. 35. Effects with pile.

FEEDING PILE YARN ONTO WARP

Ways in which the pile yarn can be fed onto the warp yarn for knot tying:

1. WITH PRECUT LENGTHS OF YARN. The best way to determine the length to be precut is to make a knot on the warp to the height of the pile desired, take it out, and use it as a guide to cutting others. Several lengths can be cut at one time by wrapping the yarn around a piece of stiff cardboard measured and cut in girth equivalent to the length of each knot; or by winding yarn around two nails set into a board the proper distance apart to give the right length for the knot. This system is particularly helpful when you want constant changes in one row of pile, such as color or height variations.

2. WITH A CONTINUOUS LENGTH OF PILE YARN CUT AFTER EACH KNOT IS TIED. This continuous length can come from (a) a cone or ball; or (b) a butterfly. The knots can be cut with scissors, razor blade, or other sharp instrument.

38

(a) In the cone or ball system, yarn from skeins, cones or balls equivalent in number to the strands of yarn per knot is bunched together and wound onto a single cone or ball. This cone or ball is then suspended from the loom or put into a box or other container in such a manner that the yarn can feed freely and continuously.

(b) In the butterfly system, yarn coming from skeins, cones or balls equivalent in number to the strands of yarn per knot is bunched together and wound as follows: with the palm of your hand (left hand for the right-handed) facing you, place and hold the end of the bunched continuous yarn between index and middle fingers (end should be facing the back of your hand). With the other hand, bring the yarn around the back of the thumb, in front of thumb, across the open palm between the ring and little fingers, back of the little finger, across the palm to back of the

thumb; and continue doing this until the hank of wound yarn is no bigger than can be comfortably handled while making knots. You will gradually get to know what size hank or butterfly is comfortable for you to handle. Cut the yarn free from the continuous flow, leaving about 6 inches dangling. (If the yarn is coming from only one skein, cone or ball, reel off lengths of yarn equivalent in number to the strands desired in the butterfly, bunch them together, and wind until only 6 inches are left.) Release the ends being held by index and middle fingers and let them hang behind your thumb. Pick up the ends left dangling and wind them tightly, but not too tightly, around the middle of the hank held between thumb and little finger 4 or 5 times and secure with a slipknot. The end of yarn placed between your index and middle fingers is the end from which you start tying knots. When gently

FIG. 36. Beginning the butterfly, made with 3 strands of yarn coming from 3 skeins feeding from a swift.

FIG. 37. The completed butterfly, with cut-off end of strands being wrapped around its middle.

39

FIG. 38. The completed butterfly. Cut-off end slipknotted after having been wrapped around the butterfly.

pulled as the knots are being tied, the yarn will automatically keep feeding from the butterfly until used up. If, as sometimes happens, the butterfly gets a little ruffled, it can be remade.

3. WITH A CONTINUOUS LENGTH OF PILE YARN CUT ONLY AFTER A WHOLE SERIES OF KNOTS IS TIED. The yarn can be fed by butterflies. In this method, the cone or ball system cannot be used; the yarn must be fed from a continuous length of yarn with two free ends which can easily pass under and over the warp ends. This, incidentally, is the only way to get a knotted pile loop; it doesn't have to come from a butterfly, but it must come from a continuous length of yarn or there could be no loop.

A pile guide, often called a "flossa stick," is usually used with this system of feeding pile yarn onto the warp. It is a wooden or metal stick, grooved on top, under and over which the pile yarn is brought after each knot is tied. When the knots are completed, the pile can be cut all at once by drawing a razor blade, Stanley knife, or other sharp instrument across the groove of the stick. If some

of the pile is to remain looped, those particular knots are left uncut and the stick pulled out. These guides are usually about ³⁄₁₆ of an inch thick and can be made in varying heights and lengths. They can be purchased already made from certain weaving equipment suppliers, or the sticks can be bought and grooved at a local lumber yard to your specifications. Angle-edged aluminum strips which can be pressed together are easy to get in any hardware store and work quite well; they too can be bought in various heights and lengths. The height of the guides determines the height of the pile. The groove for cutting at the top of the stick is usually about ¼ inch deep. More than one guide can be used in a single row of pile, either of the same or of different heights or lengths. Some people prefer to use short sticks; others prefer to use some the full width of the rug.

The pile guide can be a very useful tool when a horizontal loom is being used —the pull of gravity and the position of the guide in relation to the hands makes it cumbersome and unwieldy when used with a vertical loom. Interestingly enough, many centuries ago—and this was probably just one of many such instances—an ambitious Near East agent tried to compel the weavers in some of his establishments to use such a stick in order to cut down on the waste of yarn that occurred when knots were made and then cut separately by knife. No matter how skilled the weaver's eye or aim, some of the knots were bound to be longer than others and the trimming after the rug was finished resulted in waste. The stick did cut the waste down by about one-fourth, but slowed the weavers down so that they not only became irritated, but also lost precious piece time for which they were not paid. They rebelled, and the system was abolished. When using this feeding method with a vertical loom, it is better to use a finger as a guide to the length of loop between knots. When a row of knots is completed, the loops of the knots

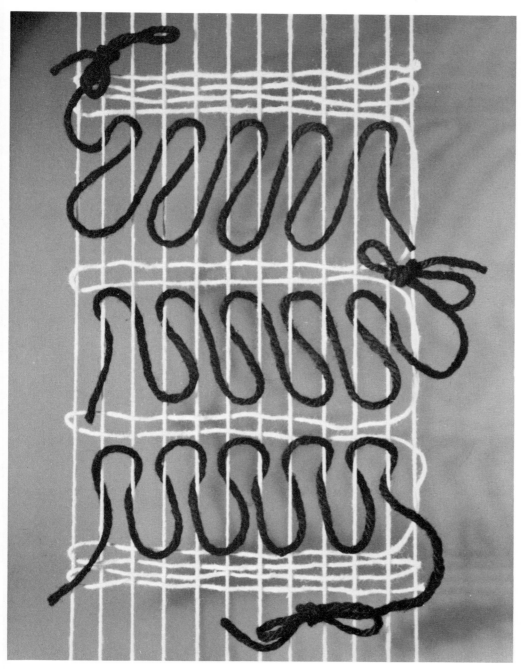

FIG. 39. Knots made with continuous yarn without a pile guide. *From bottom up:*
Ghiordes, left Sehna, right Sehna.

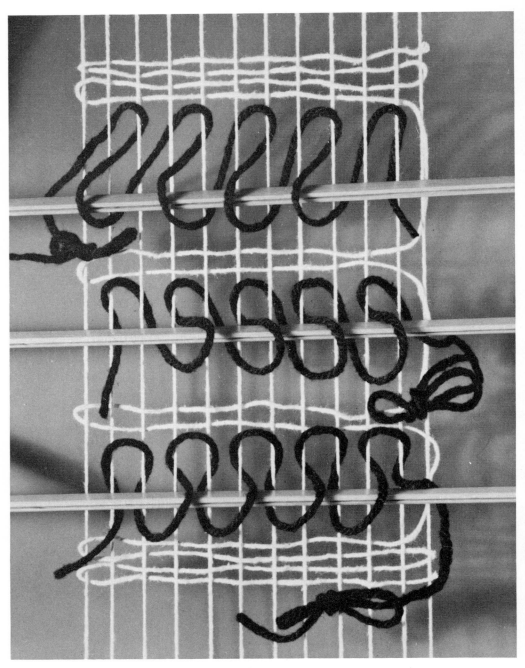

Fig. 40. Knots made with continuous yarn with a pile guide. *From bottom up:* Ghiordes, left Sehna, right Sehna.

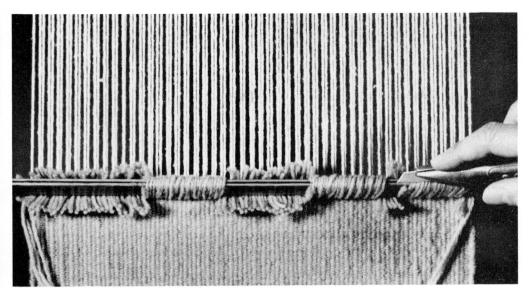

FIG. 41. One row of pile using a pile guide. Knots cut and uncut.

which are to become cut pile can be cut with scissors. This can be done on the horizontal loom also, if one prefers not to use the pile guide.

Illustrations for this are, of necessity, grossly exaggerated so that exactly what happens can be seen without question. The knots are wrapped firmly around the warp ends and the loops are wrapped firmly around the pile guide. The guide is held close to the last pick of weaving in a perpendicular position, groove side up. It is helpful when making the knot with the right hand to pick up the warp ends with the thumb and index finger of left hand, to hold the yarn of the first half of the knot against the guide with the middle finger, and with the other hand to make the other half of the knot and pull butterfly under the guide close to the weaving. After the first few knots are tied, the guide usually stands up by itself and both hands are free for knots.

Verbally stated, the rhythm or movement of the yarn when pile is looped, or left uncut until a whole series of knots is tied, is as follows:

GHIORDES WITHOUT PILE GUIDE: *Under and over left end; over and under right end; loop; and repeat from*.

GHIORDES WITH PILE GUIDE: *Under and over left end; over and under right end; under guide toward weaving; over guide away from weaving; and repeat from*.

RIGHT SEHNA: WITHOUT PILE GUIDE: *Under and over right end; under left end; loop; and repeat from*. *With pile guide:* *Under and over right end; under left end; under guide toward weaving; over guide away from weaving; and repeat from*.

LEFT SEHNA: WITHOUT PILE GUIDE: *Under and over left end; under right end; loop; and repeat from*. *With pile guide:* *Under and over left end; under right end; under guide toward weaving; over guide away from weaving; repeat from*.

KNOTS PER INCH

The number of knots—Ghiordes, Sehna, or single-warp—which will be required to make a rug depends upon (1) density of pile desired and (2) the design to be executed.

Density of pile is dependent upon the number of tufts of yarn within a given space. If the design calls for thick, lush

43

pile which stands up almost straight, there will have to be more tufts of pile per square inch than if it calls for sparse pile lying closer to the floor. If the design calls for thick and thin areas, the number of tufts will have to vary within specific areas of the rug. The number of tufts per square inch can be achieved quickly with few knots or slowly with many knots, depending upon the number and thickness of strands of pile yarn making up each separate knot. Since density of pile can be built up 3, 4, or more times as quickly by using 3, 4, or more strands of yarn per knot than by using a single strand of the same yarn in 3, 4, or more knots within the same space—and just as effectively— it would seem advisable to use more strands per knot and make fewer knots.

However, the design to be executed is another matter. There must be at least enough knots per inch to cover all the details of the design within that inch because each change has to be interpreted by a knot. Regardless of the number of strands used per knot, the more detailed a design, the more knots there will have to be. The obvious way to control this, then, is to design with less detail so that fewer knots per square inch will be required, thus lessening the time necessary to make a rug. This may sound arbitrary, but a better design will result because fine details tend to get lost in rugs. Oh, yes, some Orientals are magnificent and the details are quite clear, but consider the months required to tie thousands of knots! And, besides, isn't it a bit foolish to design in the past and not within the idiom of our time?

In designing for today's pace, it is far better most of the time to fit the design within a plan of a specific number of knots per inch and rely upon several strands per knot to build up the pile more rapidly. Except in a few cases, it will be found that 3 or 4 knots per horizontal inch are sufficient if made with the proper number of strands to produce pile of desired density. It is difficult to say how many knots per vertical inch would normally be adequate —so much depends upon the height of pile and the thickness desired. An average of about 3 knots per vertical inch is usually a good number. As to the number of strands of yarn per knot, again this is difficult to establish firmly—so much depends upon what kinds and sizes of yarns are put together in each separate knot, and the mood of the design. If the strands of pile yarn per knot are too thick, it may result in lumps underfoot and loose construction; if too thin, it might have a skimpy look. When working with Persian rug wool only, a good average is 3 or 4 strands per knot.

While the figures given here may be of some help as a starting point, they should not necessarily be your yardstick. The best guide is always a sample on the loom.

TRANSLATING PAPER DESIGN INTO KNOTS

Because designs for the knotted pile rug—and many other rugs discussed in this book—are of a variety akin to prints, the medium for their development is usually achieved by sketching on paper. Whether the sketch is developed through pencil doodlings or drawings, paper cutouts or yarn outlines, the design should finally emerge in full scale on heavy paper cut to the size and shape of the rug. Otherwise there can be no accurate visualization of what the completed rug will look like— unless the design is a small-patterned overall repeat. But our concern at the moment is not how to go about developing a design (see Aids to the Planning or Designing of Rugs, pp. 146–55). It is rather with its transition from a paper drawing into rug knots.

There are many types of designs, but all are composed of straight lines, curved lines, or a combination of the two. All can be followed on the loom by one means or another.

Straight-line designs—the ones in which

44

the motif or motifs run in horizontal, vertical, and even diagonal lines—present no special problem. They can be followed quite simply by counting off and making the number of knots that will fit within the corresponding horizontal measurements of the design and also by counting off and making the number of vertical knots which will fit within the corresponding vertical measurements of the design— or by measuring the vertical proportions with a tape measure, particularly if you have not yet done enough weaving to produce a consistent number of knots per vertical inch.

For example, let us assume the design is a simple one of 4-inch squares, green alternating with gold. The warp is made up of 8 ends per inch, resulting in 4 Ghiordes knots per horizontal inch; the rows of pile are to be spaced so that there will be 3 knots per vertical row. The pile in each horizontal row will consist of 4 inches x 4 knots per inch, or *16 green knots* alternating with 4 inches x 4 knots per inch, or *16 gold knots*. Since these are 4 x 4 inch squares, this row of knots will be repeated until 4 inches are woven; or, if you prefer, for 4 inches x 3 knots per vertical inch, or *12 rows of knots*. The next 4 inches (or 12 rows of knots) of the rug will alternate; therefore begin with horizontal rows of 16 gold knots alternating with 16 green knots and continue in this manner for 12 rows of pile, or 4 vertical inches.

Geometric designs, stripes, certain textures or overall repeats usually come under the category of the type of rug design which can be translated to the loom by measuring.

For designs which do not lend themselves to easy translation by measurement, there are several ways in which they can be followed:

1. By drawing the design on the warp when it is set up ready to weave and after the preliminary weaving which is done at the beginning of any piece to stabilize the warp. This can be done by making a stiff paper stencil of the full scale design, or by cutting it out gradually section by section, and tracing the design carefully on the warp itself with pen and ink or with a felt-tipped ink marker. Unless the rug is a small one with the warp completely exposed and none of it wound around the warp beam, the design will have to be drawn on the warp in sections as the rug progresses. Make sure that the ink penetrates the warp ends or the motion of the beater and the constant handling of the ends may erase the marks. If this begins to happen, the spots can, of course, be touched up.

2. It is sometimes possible to roll the design along with the finished portions of the rug over the breast and cloth beams of a horizontal loom, and to follow it in that manner through the openings between the warp ends. However, this method is subject to slippage, so if the design is at all complicated, it is not recommended; but it is quite suited to the vertical loom because the design can hang in the back of the loom undisturbed, with only enough space between to allow for comfortable handling of the warp.

3. By using graph paper as a guide. Perhaps the easiest way to do this is to mark off the full-scale design in squares equal to the planned number of knots per horizontal and vertical inch. If you prefer not to mark up the design itself, tracing paper can be squared off and laid over the design. This will isolate the lines or contours of the design into separate squares, each one equivalent to a knot. This could be used as the guide, but it might be easier to handle regular downscaled graph paper. It then becomes a simple matter of transferring each knot to its proper square on the smaller graph paper and indicating by a symbol in that square what that knot should be. If it's only a matter of color change, the knots can be x'd in with the color of the knot; otherwise some other coding can identify what each knot should be.

Since the rug is made from the bottom

up, the graph paper should be followed accordingly. The bottom row of squares will be the first row of knots in the rug; the second row of squares from the bottom, the second row of knots, etc. You should be careful to weave as close to the same number of knots per vertical inch as planned, otherwise there will be a distortion of design. There is no such problem horizontally because the ends are fixed in number, as well as by the reed which confines them within a certain measurement.

THE LOOM

The equivalent of a 2-harness floor loom is all that is required to make the knotted woven rug, because the weaving that holds the pile in place and forms the foundation of the rug is plain weave. A loom with more harnesses can, of course, be used. It does not need to have been especially constructed to make rugs, though one that is good and sturdy with a heavy beater is very desirable.

It may be horizontal or vertical. No other loom equipment is necessary with the horizontal loom because the beater is already attached to the loom. With the vertical loom—unless it is the type that is really the same as a horizontal loom tilted to an almost vertical position—it is necessary to have a hand beater. This is very much like an enlarged comb made of heavy metal, often about 4 inches wide and 4 inches long, with about 4 teeth per inch. It has a down-angled handle which makes it easier for the force of the beat to go downward where the filling belongs. With the hand beater it is necessary to beat across the rug several times, whereas with the horizontal beater it can be done all at once with a firm pull or two of the beater. The horizontal loom is more convenient and efficient to work with than the vertical loom. Shuttles and butterflies can find an easy resting place on top of the finished portion of the rug, a pile guide can be used to speed up the tying of the

knots, a wider shed can usually be obtained, and it is easier to shoot a shuttle through an open shed from that position. On the other hand, a vertical loom takes up less floor space, is often less expensive to buy, and can more easily be made by the home carpenter—sometimes, but not always, at less cost.

THE WARP

This should be made of strong, plied yarn because it forms part of the foundation of the rug which must be sturdy enough to last and hold to the floor. It should be firm, with not too much stretch, and fairly smooth but not slippery. A good grade of cord, the kind available on cones at most paper and twine stores, is inexpensive and most frequently used. It is easy on the hands and holds the knots firmly without allowing them to slip out of place. Linen which is also very good is a bit more expensive but more attractive visually. The visual quality of the warp yarn should be considered if it is to show at the ends of the rug as fringe; if not, its visual quality is secondary to its wearing and weaving properties.

The number of ends per inch varies with the number and thickness of knots per inch desired, though most rug weavers usually make their designs conform to a more or less constant number of ends per inch. It will be found that the large majority of rug designs will lend themselves well to interpretation on a 3- or 4-knots-per-inch warp. Since it usually requires 2 ends to make a knot, a 3-knots-per-horizontal-inch rug would require 6 ends per inch; a 4-knots-per-horizontal-inch rug would require 8 ends per inch.

With a 6-ends-per-inch warp, cotton cord of 12- or 14-ply weaves well; with 8 ends per inch, 8- or 10-ply cotton cord weaves well. A warp with heavy yarn usually requires fewer ends per inch and can take more thickness of yarn per knot than can a warp made of finer yarn.

When making up the warp, there should

be at least 2 extra ends added because the ends on either side of the rug are not used for knotting. Some weavers like to leave 2 ends free of knots on either side of the rug, both ends usually working as one.

THE FILLING

As you discovered in the section on **KNOTS**, the pile is attached to the warp. It does not interlace with it and therefore does not form part of the weave. In order to hold the pile in place and to hold the rug together, rows of plain weaving must be inserted between rows of knots. Unless the filling is intended to show as part of the design, there should be no more filling between rows than each succeeding row of knots can generously cover. Generally speaking, each row of pile should at least cover the loops of the actual knotted section of the previous pile row, and preferably more. Otherwise, the pressure of people walking on the rug could easily result in exposing the backing which, though attractive in its functionalism, is not particularly so aesthetically. The number of picks of filling between pile rows is determined by the thickness and height of the pile. If the pile is to be short, there should be fewer picks of filling between knotted rows than if the pile is to be long. If the pile is to be dense, there should be fewer picks of filling between rows of pile than if the pile is to be sparse.

The plain weave in the rug should not be interrupted by the insertion of the pile row. If the pick just previous to a pile row was in a shed with *odd* ends up, the pick right after the pile row should be with *even* ends up. An easy way to remember which pick was last—odd or even ends up—is to have the shuttle work in synchronization with the treadles. When the shed worked with the left treadle is used, the shuttle is shot from left to right; when the shed worked with the right treadle is used, the shuttle is shot from right to left. Automatically, therefore, after a row of knots, if the shuttle is on the right of the rug, you will know that the right treadle should be used; if the shuttle is on the left of the work, the left treadle should be used.

A too tightly twisted cord should be avoided as filling because it will twist into knots as the shuttle is being shot through the shed; and it is apt to cause boardiness which would nullify one of the pile rug's most valuable qualities—rich visual and underfoot softness. If the filling is not to be part of the design, the same kind of cotton cord suggested for the warp can be used. If the filling is to show, the design would determine the kind of yarn to be used.

At the beginning and end of each rug, a webbing or hem of some sort which will remain as part of the rug is necessary to hold the first and last rows of pile in place. If it is to show when the rug is ready for the floor, it might be preferable to weave it of one of the yarns forming the pile. If it is to be turned under, it is up to the weaver's judgment what kind of yarn should be used—cotton cord, or more decorative yarn. What the length of those hems will be if they are to show is again up to the weaver's discretion. It must be remembered that anything that shows on the floor should be considered as part of the design and treated accordingly. If the hem is to be turned under, there need be no more than an amount adequate to make a generous hem; it is usually finished off inside with rug tape.

Bubbling

The plain weave which holds the knots in place should, if one desires a strong backing, cover the warp completely. This is most easily done by "bubbling" which distributes the yarn more generously than just laying it between the shed in a straight line. It also helps to keep the rug at its intended width because it prevents the edges from pulling in.

To **bubble**: open the shed, shoot the

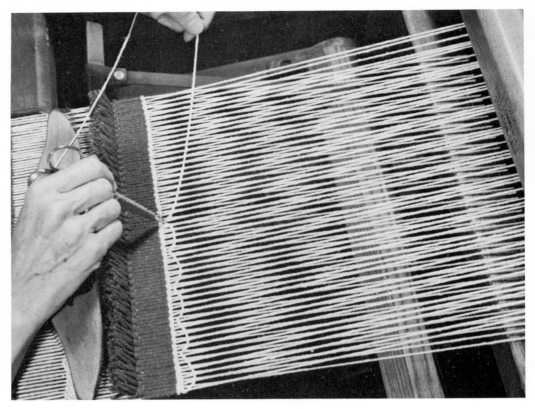

FIG. 42. One row of filling being "bubbled."

shuttle across, holding the filling yarn at a slight upward diagonal so that there will be enough slack to enable you to make bubbles. With the shed still open, bubble or scallop the yarn by pushing it toward the weaving every 1½ inches or so with your fingers or the point of small, pointed scissors, whichever is easier for you—scissors seem to work faster than a finger for some people. Close the shed; beat hard; change the shed and beat again. Repeat the bubbling with each pick until the desired number of picks have been inserted.

In making the bubbles, it is best not to indent them too deeply or little lumps of filling will form which have a tendency to loosen the firmness of the weave—the point of each bubble should barely touch the last pick of weaving.

The same technique can, and with certain rugs should, be applied to the weaving of the hems at either end of the rug.

If perchance the rug should start building up on one side more than the other, or in the middle more than on the sides, this should be corrected by making bubbles farther apart on the lower side or sides until both sides become even. Straight, unbubbled picks build up more quickly than the bubbled, because they do not weave as closely. Continue even bubbling after the correction has been made.

THE EDGES

The first and the last ends of the warp are not used for tying knots because the edge knots would not be as firmly in place as the others, the loop of the knot would be exposed, and therefore those knots would wear out more quickly. To make up for the absence of knots, to make the edges stronger, and to finish them more decoratively should the edges

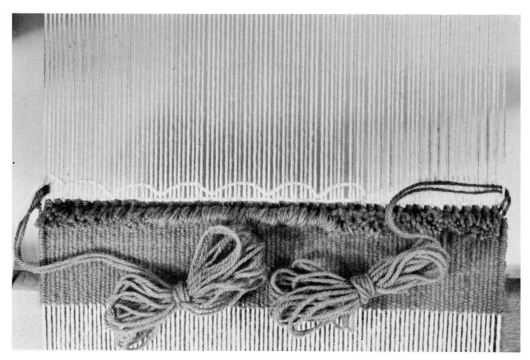

FIG. 43. Wrapping of edge yarns at the insertion point of each pick.

be exposed when the rug is on the floor, continuous lengths of pile yarn are carried along and wrapped around either side of the rug. This yarn is most easily fed by a butterfly inserted into each edge of the weaving just before or right after the first row of pile knots. These butterflies are made up of as many strands of pile yarn (usually 2 strands are sufficient) as will fully cover the weaving along the selvages. They are wrapped around the outer warp end and the loop formed at the insertion point of each pick. In other words, the right butterfly is used after a pick has been inserted from the right side, and the left butterfly is used after a pick has been inserted from the left side. Every so often it may be necessary to wrap the yarn around more than once to cover the edge more fully, but there must not be so much extra yarn that the edges curl—the whole of the foundation should lie flat on the floor. Just before the last row of pile is inserted, the edge yarn is woven into the warp for about an inch, and the butterflies cut off.

Some weavers like to use 2 ends woven as one on each side of the rug to form this edge. This makes the edges a little thicker, but the wrapping is done exactly the same way as described except that it encircles 2 ends at once instead of one. Various other methods of wrapping or finishing edges have been and are used, but this is as effective as any and much faster than most.

CHAPTER 4

Finishing the Woven Rug

Unless the ends of the rug are to play an important part in the design of the rug, the ends of a woven rug are usually finished quite unobtrusively; otherwise they would vie with the design of the rug. The two usual ways of finishing them off are:

FRINGING

1. Fringing the warp, or applying fringe to the rug
   (a) by taking 2 or 3 warp ends together and knotting them in place as close to the weaving as possible with a simple overhand knot,
   (b) by braiding a number of warp ends together for a few inches and tying them together with an overhand knot as close to the end of the braid as possible,
   (c) by making any of the more decorative fringes which in themselves are forms of knotting techniques,
   (d) by making fringe of one of the pile yarns on the loom as the rug is being woven by tying long Ghiordes knots to the warp: at the beginning of the rug, right after the rug hem and just 2 picks or so before the first pile row of the body of the rug; at the end of the rug, 1 or 2 picks after the last pile row of the body of the rug, and just before the finishing hem is woven. The knots making up the fringe at the end

FIG. 44. Finishing the rug—various methods. (*1*) Tapestry weave hem, one light alternating with one dark pick. Warp ends tied into overhand knots. (*2*) Tapestry weave hem. *Left-hand side:* 2 ends together plaited into a 3-part braid. *Right-hand side:* Another type of fancy overhand knotted fringe. (*3*) Long fringe tied into the rug as it is being made. The *bottom section* represents the beginning of the rug, fringe tied with Ghiordes knot; *top section,* end of the rug, fringe tied with reverse Ghiordes knot. Four ends are used for knotting fringe on the left side, 2 ends for that on the right side. *4, 5, 6:* Three steps to finishing the rug with turned-under hem: (*4*) Preliminary weaving taken out sectionally, every 2 ends tied together with a square knot, after which excess "fringe" is cut off. (*5*) Sewing tape onto the front of the rug and over and along square-knotted ends. (*6*) The hem turned under, and the other edge of the tape sewed onto the back of 'the rug. This last also shows the type of fringe made by sewing strands of yarn into the edge of the turned-under hem and overhand-knotted in place.

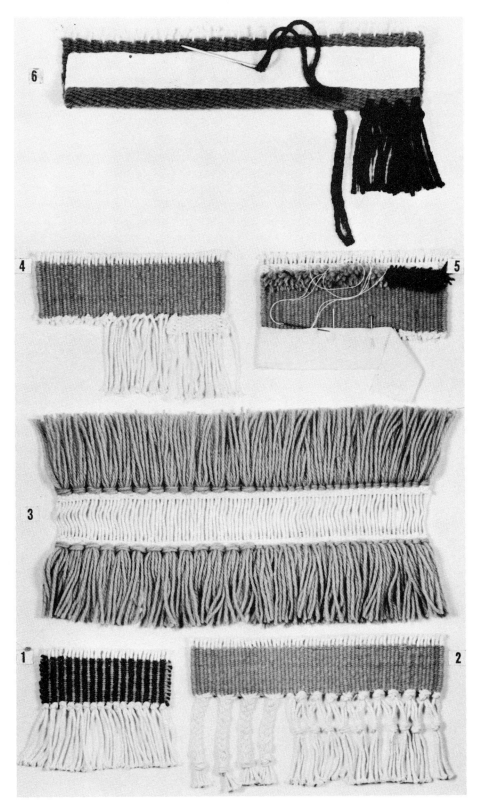

of the rug will have to be reversed (see page 53, Reversed Ghiordes Knot). When this method is used, the hem is turned under and hemmed as described hereafter.

Pile fringe can also be sewed into the finished hem of a rug. Thread a blunt-ended needle with the desired number of strands of pile yarn, insert into the rug hem leaving long ends at front and back of rug. Hold the ends together and knot them in place with an overhand knot as close to the edge of the rug as possible.

HEMMING

Starting from one edge of the rug and continuing all the way across the warp, tie 2 ends together with a square knot as close to the weaving as possible until all ends are square-knotted. Trim the warp ends to about $\frac{1}{4}$ of an inch. From the right side of the rug, pin one edge of rug tape (preferably dyed to match color of hemming) to the hem, just covering the square knots, and stitch. Turn the hem under, pin it in place, and sew the other side of the tape to the back of the rug. Good strong thread should be used with stitches that do not show.

In hemming, it is preferable to leave at least a slight bit of the hem showing on the face of the rug—otherwise the first and last rows of knots will fall away from the rug and form an unattractive split. And, too, the foundation may show.

When cutting off the rug from either end of the loom be sure that enough warp is left to finish the rug comfortably in the way you want to finish it. This may seem a foolish warning, but it has happened enough times to warrant this warning: trying to work with short ends of warp can be quite frustrating and it is really unnecessary.

In all kinds of weaving, including rugs, the ends of a warp have to be pulled in place with some sort of preliminary weaving before the actual piece is begun. If, after cutting the rug off the loom, this preliminary weaving is taken out all at once, by the time all the warp ends are fringed or square-knotted in place, some part of the hem of the rug will have started coming out of place. This can be avoided—and therefore the finishing made much easier—by cutting out and pulling out the preliminary weaving, and finishing the warp ends in small sections at a time. Several picks of weaving to be pulled out in the same way should also be woven at the end of the rug. Or—and you might find this even easier to handle, particularly if the warp ends are to be square-knotted for a turned-under hem—the end of the rug might be finished right on the loom by cutting the warp off gradually a few ends at a time and square-knotting them close to the hem, working first one side and then the other side, alternating back and forth evenly toward the middle. Unfortunately, this cannot be done comfortably at the beginning of the rug.

52

CHAPTER 5

Experiments with Knots

There are other variations in the technique of knotting which have not turned up in the literature in any research I have done, but which I have developed out of sheer necessity to find a way to achieve a certain texture, or express a certain idea. Basically, the knots used to get the desired results have been one of the three standard knots, but with variations in their use. These variations you may wish to share with me. It is hoped that it will help stimulate you into doing some experimenting of your own. The following are but a few of the effects which one can get by manipulating the pile technique.

DIRECTIONAL PILE
Reversed Ghiordes

So far we have seen that the pile formed by knots already handed down to us can lie in 3 directions—south, east, and west. Why can it not also fall in a fourth, or northward direction? It can readily be seen that the only knot with which this can be done is the Ghiordes made upside down, or in reverse. The only difference between tying this and the standard Ghiordes knot is that the two ends of the knot come together toward the unfinished part of the rug, rather than toward the weaving. Because it falls toward unwoven warp, it has a tendency to come apart and needs the support of at least one row

of filling before it will stand by itself. When a pile guide is used, this is no problem—the knots are left on the stick until at least one row of filling is inserted before the pile is cut or before the stick is removed if the pile is to be kept looped. If no pile guide is used, the falling apart tendency can be counteracted by making only a few knots at a time and gradually inserting a pick of filling to hold them in place.

When a pile guide is used, the rhythm of movement for making the reversed Ghiordes knot is: **First Knot**—insert the pile yarn from the right of, and under and over the left-hand end of the 2 warp ends necessary to make the knot, and to the right of and under the right-hand end, bringing the loop of the knot close to the weaving, the ends of the knot facing the unwoven warp; bring the yarn under the pile guide toward the weaving.

Second Knot—loop yarn from the front of and over the pile guide toward the back of the loom, insert from the right of, and under and over the left-hand end of the next pair of warp ends; bring through loop and under pile guide toward and close to the weaving; insert from right of and under the right-hand end, and under the stick toward the weaving. Repeat with the second knot until the desired number of reversed knots are completed.

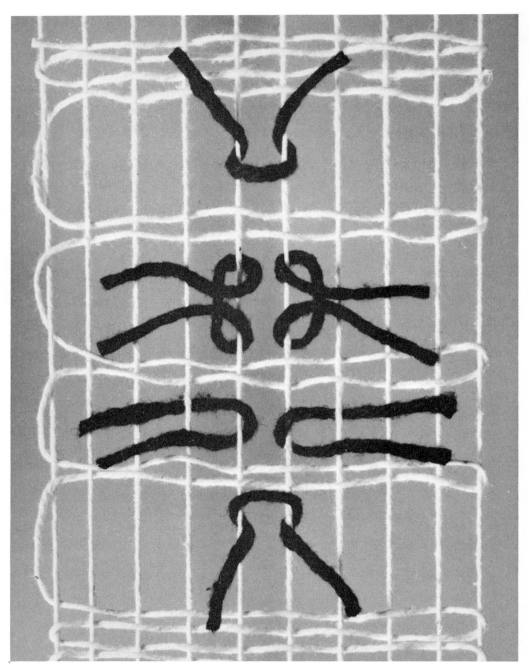

FIG. 45. Knots lying in 4 directions. *From bottom up:* Ghiordes knot. *Row 2:* At left, right-hand Sehna; at right, left-hand Sehna. *Row 3:* Left, looped knot made by bringing the ends of a looped strand of yarn under, over, and through the loop at the left of the warp end; right, the ends of the looped strand of yarn brought under, over, and through the loop at the right of the warp end. *Row 4:* Reversed Ghiordes knot.

FIG. 46. Detail of striped flat rug, with Ghiordes, left and right Sehna, and reversed Ghiordes knots forming a flowerlike pile design.

The above and following photos show this device used in two separate ways. The first design makes use of all four directions of pile for its flowerlike clusters; the second is the Ghiordes right-side up and upside-down, or reversed, with both cut and looped pile, giving a zigzag effect. In the rug shown in the color illustration 1, a detail of which is shown here, the Ghiordes knot is used in the same manner as in the latter example.

Looped Pile

If the direction of cut pile can go all around the compass, why can't looped pile do the same thing? It can. The only difference in technique is that the strands of yarn, or butterfly, must be carried along from horizontal row to horizontal row of knots instead of from knot to knot as in the standard looped pile.

STRIPES

Let us assume that a single row of upward or vertical loops ½ inch apart is to form a part of the design. A butterfly is attached to the warp by means of a knot at the beginning of the vertical loop stripe. The butterfly is dropped and the rug built up in whatever manner is necessary to the execution of the design for ½ inch. The butterfly is once more picked up and looped and knotted into the rug, not to be picked up again until the next ½ inch is woven; and so on until the stripe is completed. If this stripe is to be 6 rows wide, 6 butterflies will be needed, one for each row so that the loops can be continuous from row to row.

55

FIG. 47. Detail of a cut and looped pile rug made with Ghiordes and reversed Ghiordes knots.

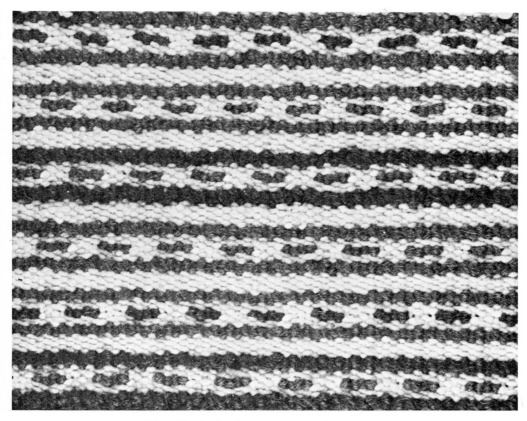

FIG. 48. Back of the rug shown in Fig. 47.

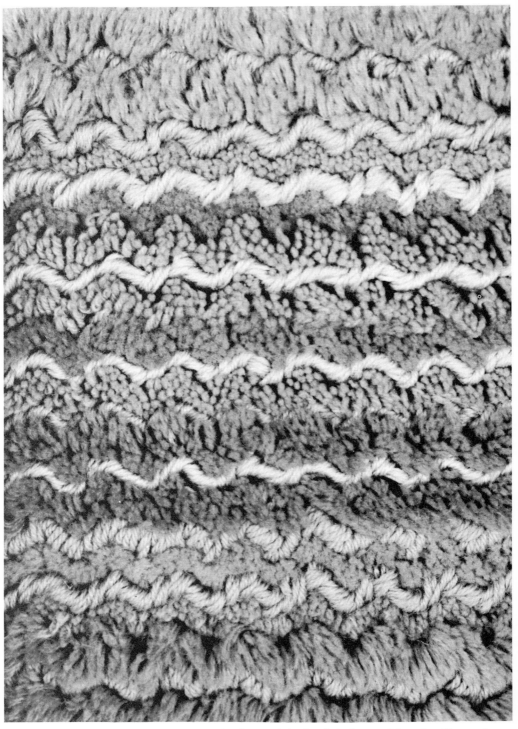

FIG. 49. Detail of the rug shown on the front of the book jacket and in color illustration #1. Ghiordes and reversed Ghiordes knots.

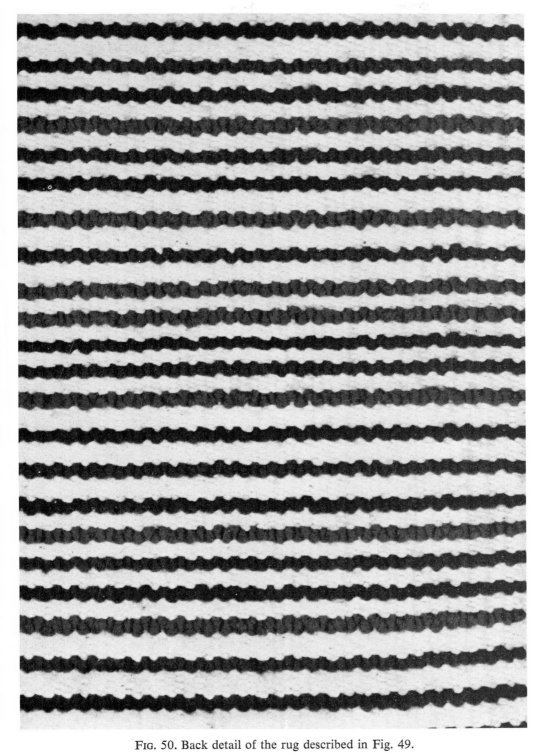

FIG. 50. Back detail of the rug described in Fig. 49.

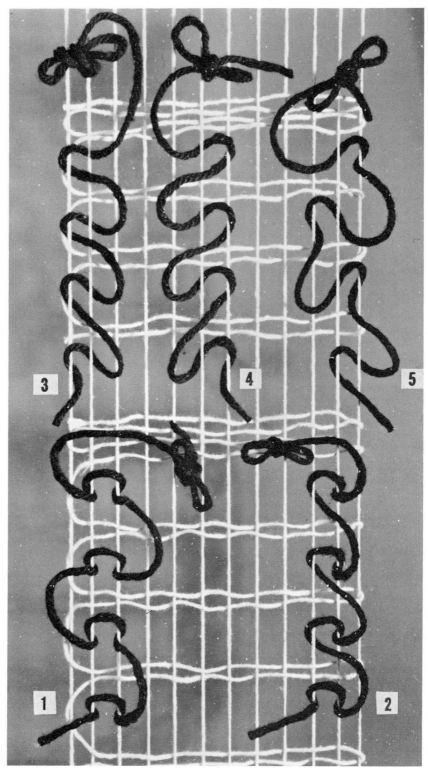

FIG. 51. Looped pile carried vertically. (*1*) Ghiordes knot tied from left to right, alternating with Ghiordes tied from right to left. (*2*) Ghiordes knots, all tied from left to right. (*3*) All left-hand Sehnas. (*4*) All right-hand Sehnas. (*5*) Left-hand Sehna alternating with right-hand Sehna.

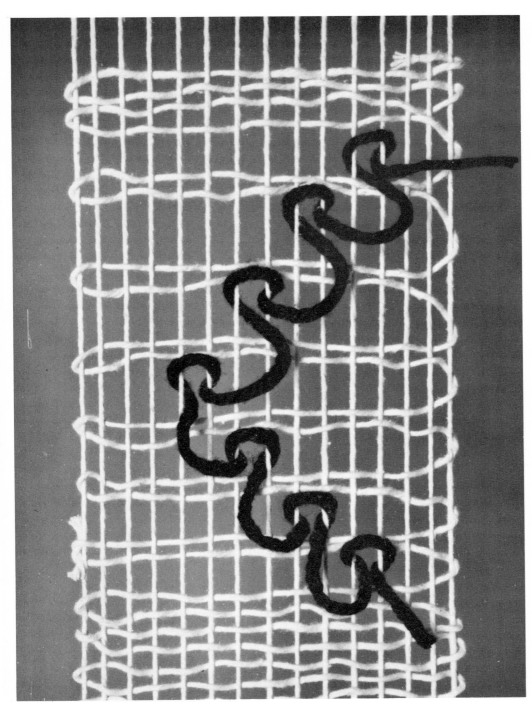

FIG. 52. Looped pile carried diagonally, forming the left side of diamond shape. *Bottom section*, Ghiordes knots tied from right to left; *top section*, Ghiordes knots tied from left to right.

If one of the 2-warp knots (Ghiordes or Sehna) is being used, you may wish to alternate tying the knots, first from left to right, and then from right to left, according to which side of the warp ends the butterfly rests. The preceding illustrations will probably make this statement clearer to you.

You may find it interesting that long after I had started using this device, I discovered the existence of the Coptic rug (Fig. 18), in which somewhat the same device was used. True, its use was different in the Coptic rug—the pile yarn was carried on the surface of the fabric from row to row for the sake of convenience in places where narrow strips of one color went in a vertical or diagonal direction. It was not looped between rows—in fact, it was hidden by the cut pile of the rug— but the germ of the idea was there.

Outlines

If the looped pile is to outline a part of the design, it can be moved on from row to row and worked in a diagonal or other direction. It cannot be worked toward the beginning, of course, but can be built up from either right or left and made to converge. Let us assume you want to outline a diamond with loops. Two butterflies would have to be carried, one for each side of the diamond. The 2 butterflies would work this way: they would start at the base of the diamond and occupy the 4 warp ends lying side by side (2, if the single warp knot were used). As the diamond progresses, the left butterfly would move over to the warp ends to left of center, the right butterfly to right of center, and continue to move outward until half the diamond is completed, when they would start moving toward one another again and continue to converge until they meet at the upper point of the diamond, where they are knotted as at the beginning. The pitch of the diamond can be very steep or very gradual; it is free to progress from end to end, or from one warp end to several beyond.

For a clearer diagonal line, 2-warp knots made with the butterfly moving to the left could be tied from right to left and knots made with the butterfly moving to the right tied from left to right. Figure 52 ought to make this quite clear.

Knotted Braid

Another and slightly more complex way of extending the loop other than horizontally is to braid the yarn in a vertical or upward direction. For this, at least 3 butterflies need to be attached to the warp in side-by-side knots. To begin the braid, attach each butterfly by means of one of the knots, using 6 adjacent warp ends. Weave a few picks of plain weave— take the middle butterfly and cross over to the first butterfly's 2 warp ends, tying a knot onto those 2 warp ends; weave another few rows of filling, take the extreme left butterfly, cross the yarn over the loop formed by the middle butterfly and tie a knot on the 2 warp ends of the third butterfly. Weave a few picks more of plain weave. Take the third butterfly, cross it over the yarn of the first butterfly, and tie onto the first 2 warp ends of the braided section. Continue to cross the butterflies in this manner using the first 2 ends and the last 2 ends alternately for knotting, ignoring the 2 center ends from now on. It is only necessary to use the middle 2 ends to begin the braid with the (at least) 3 sets of yarn which are required for a braid. Needless to say, the butterflies are always crossed in a 1, 2, 3 order, with the original middle butterfly moving to the position of No. 1. If there is a doubt as to which butterfly crosses and ties next, simply take the lowest one, the one knotted closest to the beginning of the rug.

The amount of weaving done between knots depends upon the length and height of the loop. Unless an uneven length of loop is desired, the same number of picks is inserted between crossings and knots, except possibly at the very beginning. Since there are 3 butterflies and only 2

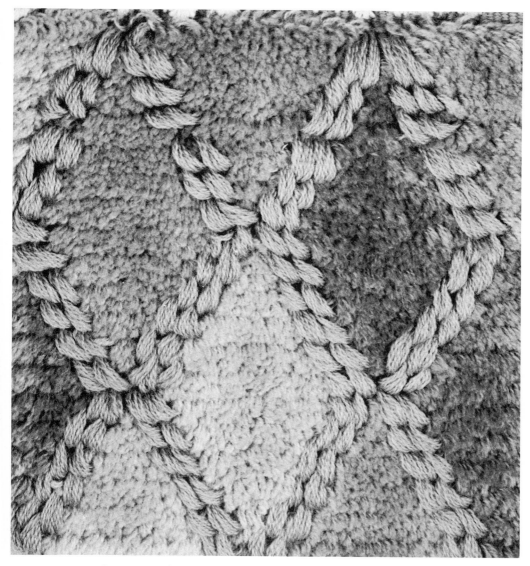

Fig. 53. Practical application of diagonally carried pile loops, left butterflies outlining the left side and right butterflies the right side of diamond-shaped motifs.

crossing points (from one edge of braid to the other), the middle butterfly has to be integrated to conform. In order to avoid one long loop at the beginning which would be required to jockey the middle one into an edge position, weave half the number of picks, loop the middle butterfly over to the left edge for knotting, weave half the number of picks again and cross the left butterfly to the extreme right. All butterflies are now on the 4 outer ends of the 6 warp ends where they should be. From then on, weave the full number of picks before continuing the braiding process.

PILE WITH SKIPPED WARP ENDS

As already mentioned, it is not necessary when using pile to make it an all-pile rug. Pile can be used in combination with flat areas to make very attractive rugs which can be less expensive as well as less time-consuming.

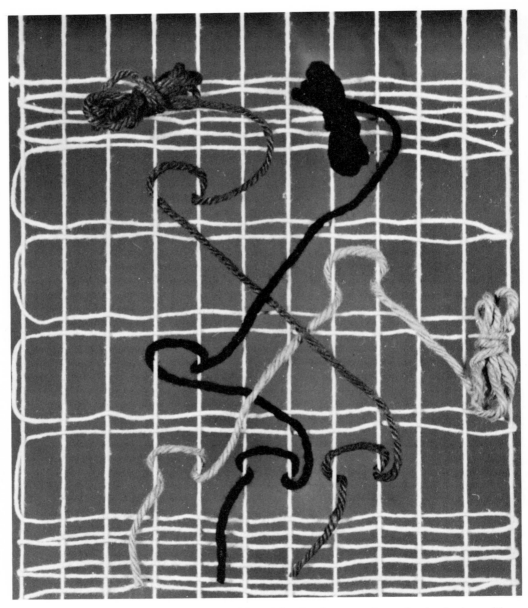

FIG. 54. Ghiordes-knotted vertical braid and its development from the beginning with 3 butterflies.

One can also make all-pile rugs, either cut or uncut, without using up all the warp ends in tying knots. By skipping warp ends, one can achieve a semisculptured effect without having to contour-clip the pile later. This can be quite effective and, even in a single-color rug, delineate contours which *are* the design. The gaps made by the areas where no knots are tied form depressions that add another dimension to the rug, which color alone could not do. In using this device one must take care that the areas without knots do not reveal the foundation section of the rug; the pile should be long enough to counteract this, or there should be fewer skipped ends.

When warp ends are skipped in making looped pile, it results in lengthening or extending the loop, not necessarily in height but in breadth. Rather interesting textural effects can occur when skipped ends are used in combination with non-skipped ends.

In this, as in all other cases where deviations from the norm are used, the foundation of the rug is apt to show through. If so, it is merely a question of using the proper filling yarn which will blend in with the surface texture.

FIG. 55. Detail of rug #2 in the color section, using Ghiordes-knotted vertical braid as part of its design motif. (Photograph by A. Burton Carnes, New York. Courtesy of *Handweaver and Craftsman* magazine.)

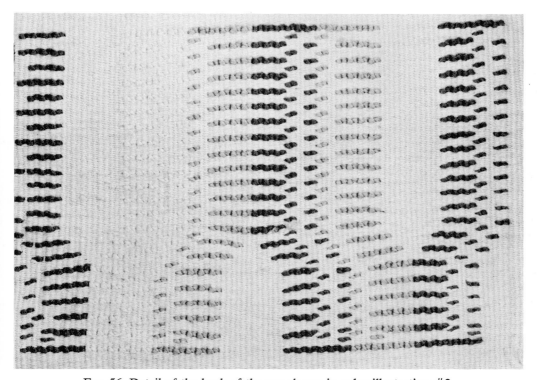

FIG. 56. Detail of the back of the rug shown in color illustration #2.

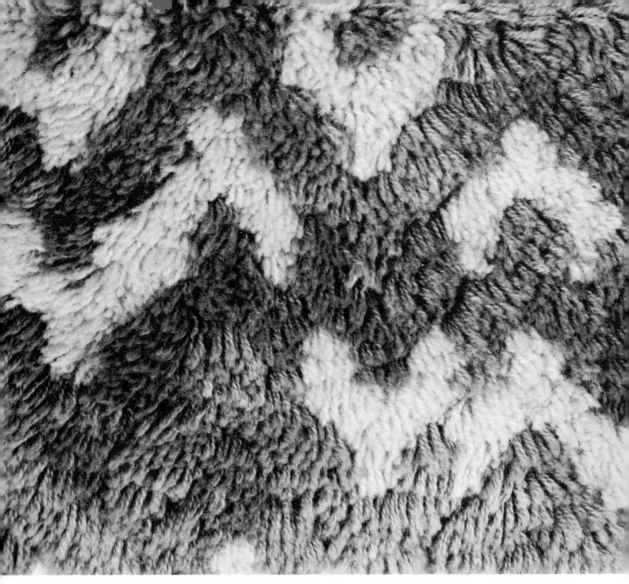

FIG. 57. Rug sample with cut pile, ends skipped in knotting, giving a semisculptured look.

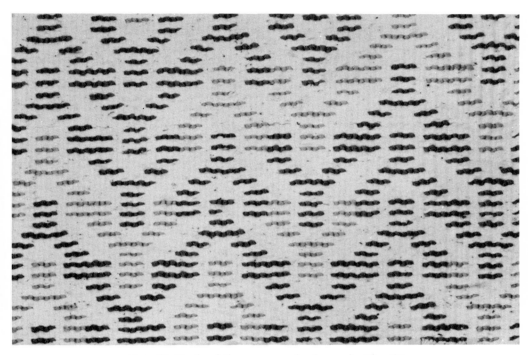

Fɪɢ. 58. Back of the rug sample shown in Fig. 57.

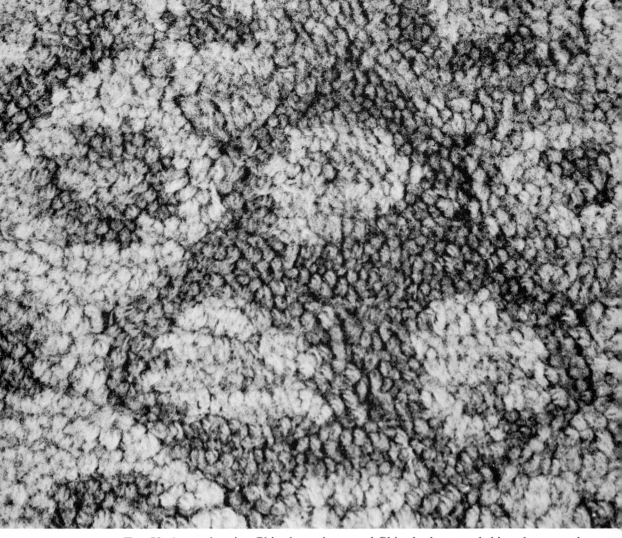

FIG. 59. A sample using Ghiordes and reversed Ghiordes knots and skipped warp ends.

FIG. 60. Back detail of the sample shown in Fig. 59.

FIG. 61. Looped pile carried horizontally, with warp ends skipped in knotting.

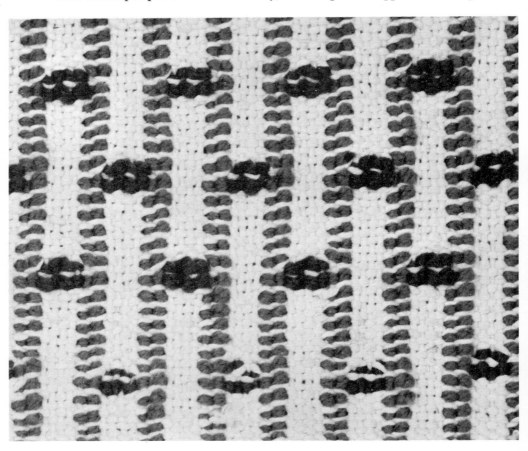

FIG. 62. Back of the sample shown in Fig. 61.

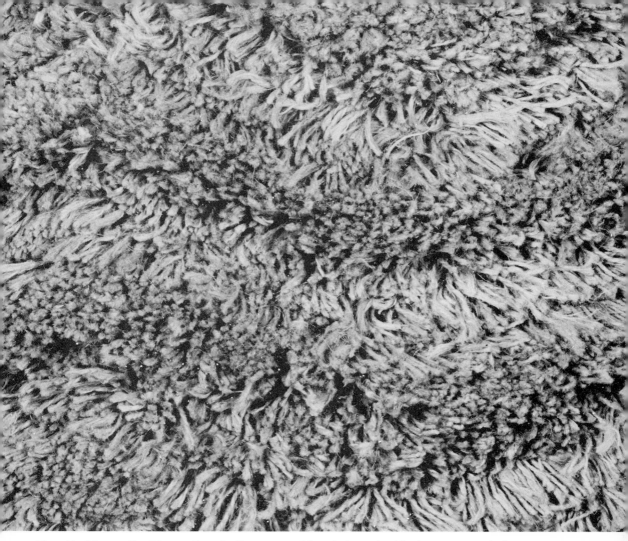

FIG. 63. Linen pile. The scalloped effect was achieved through skipping warp ends in tying knots.

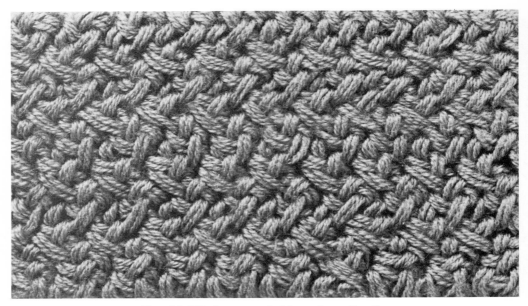

FIG. 64. Pile loops carried in various directions.

FIG. 65. Pile loops carried in various directions.

74

CHAPTER 6

Knotted Pile Without Loom

The knotted pile is sometimes applied to an already woven piece of fabric called warp cloth or duraback, or to a fabric handwoven for that purpose. The warp cloth is a heavy grade fabric woven of heavy cotton in a count of about 15 vertical by 15 horizontal threads per square inch; the duraback is the same count but woven of less heavy yarn. The handwoven fabric is sometimes woven with blended yarns and sometimes with cotton; some of it is woven with "holes" at regular intervals to facilitate the sewing of knots in those rows. The holes have the same effect as the spaces between ends when knotting the pile on the loom. Warp cloth, or other fabric without holes, is a little more flexible because knots can be tied in any of the rows of weaving; the space between the horizontal and vertical threads is the same all over the fabric.

The warp cloth comes 36 or 39 inches wide; the duraback in a variety of widths from 40 inches to over 16 feet. Since they are of square construction, the knots can be tied either across the width or across the length of the fabric. When purchasing duraback, one should figure which is the more economical to buy—a shorter yardage of wide fabric, or longer yardage of narrower fabric. In figuring the dimensions of duraback needed, one should allow enough extra in width and length

for generous hems all around the rug, to be turned under when the rug is completed. Two and a half extra inches all around will result in about a 2-inch finished hem; 3 extra inches will give a better 2½-inch completed hem. When using the handwoven fabric the knots must usually be tied horizontally—ordinarily it has a woven hem at either end, finished with fringe. It is ordered according to the dimensions of each particular rug. A 6-foot x 9-foot rug, for instance, would require a 6- x 9-foot piece of fabric, plus length of fringe.

If handwoven fabric is used, transfer the design to graph paper as described in the woven knotted rug section, page 45, and follow it row by row from bottom up, or use wax crayon or tailor's chalk to trace the design onto the fabric. If warp cloth or duraback is used, lay the fabric on a flat surface and trace the design carefully onto it in one of the ways described under the hooked rug section, page 93. It is wise to machine-stitch the non-selvage edges of warp cloth to prevent raveling which otherwise is bound to occur while making the rug.

No frame is required for this method; it is worked from the lap. To make the pile, you will need blunt-ended tapestry needles with eyes big enough to thread the strands of pile yarn used for each knot. Unless you want to be constantly thread-

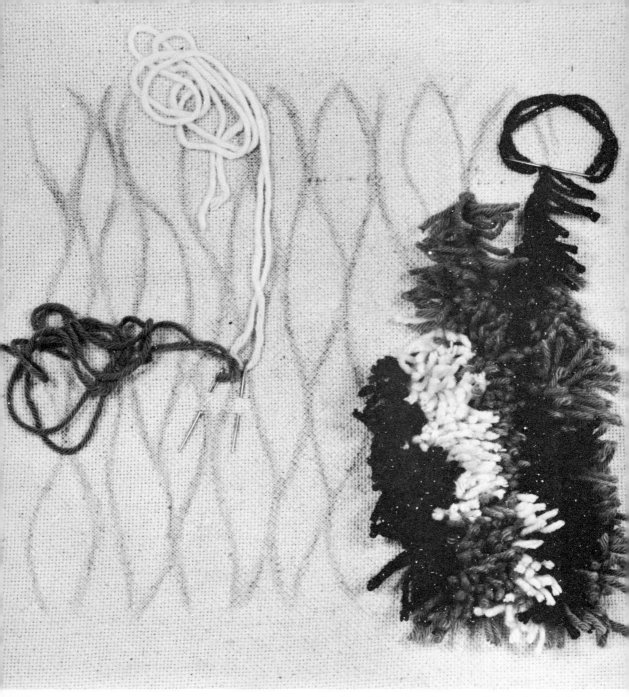

FIG. 66. Ghiordes knot sewed or embroidered into already woven foundation fabric.

ing and unthreading needles, you will need several of these if the strands of yarn in the separate knots vary considerably. The Ghiordes knot is used in this method and is made in exactly the same way as already described except that the butterfly is replaced by the threaded needle. In this case, it is definitely easier and more comfortable to use the Ghiordes than the Sehna because the "stitch" is one which progresses always in the same direction (from left to right—or right to left if one is left-handed), and in which the motion of the hand is always the same. Using a pile guide with this system is a bit awkward and also slows one down.

When using handwoven material with holes and making knots from left to right, start making pile in the first row of holes. Insert the threaded needle under and over the second end or group of ends bunched together, and over and under the third end or group of ends bunched together between holes, pulling both ends of pile toward you to the height desired. Cut, or loop pile yarn to the next knot, and repeat knotting across row. The first and last ends are not used for knotting.

When using warp cloth or duraback, the process of knotting is the same except that it is best to insert the needle under 2 threads, over 4, and under 2, simply because the threads of the warp cloth tend to pop up when only 2 threads are used for a knot.

As in the case of the woven knotted rug, this pile can vary in height, texture, and color—in height, particularly if warp cloth or its equivalent is used because one is not confined to a particular row for knotting; one can knot all over the fabric. Minimum height of the pile is predetermined with handwoven backing with holes because it must be long enough so that the backing does not show.

The rug with warp cloth or duraback foundation will need to be finished by first trimming it to about 3 inches beyond the pile all around the rug, or whatever extra cloth you have allowed. Turn excess fabric under to form a hem after turning the raw edges under. Miter the corners, cutting off any excess inside fabric, and sew the hem to the fabric with carpet thread with a blind hemstitch.

CHAPTER 7

The Woven Pile Rug Without Knots

FILLING PILE LOOPS

This system of making pile is not as secure as knotting it, but it is faster. It, too, like the knotted pile, must alternate rows of pile with picks of plain weave to hold the pile in place. There are two major types. The one like the 2500 B.C. towel of Fig. 13 is made by inserting the pile yarn as a pick of filling and pulling it into loops above the foundation of the fabric. The other, like the carpet of Fig. 18, is made by laying the pile yarn on top of the fabric and pulling it under some of the warp ends into loops above the foundation of the fabric. The latter is called the Sehna loop because it results in partially overlapping Sehna knots. Another of this type, which is slower to make, is very like the Ghiordes knot. Other variations of these exist, but they are all based on the same principles of coming through a shed, coming from on top of the warp, or occasionally coming from underneath the warp. It would seem that the first type has an advantage over the others if the loops are not cut because, while it may pull out as easily, it can't pull out as far—it's held into the fabric as a pick; but, when cut, the Sehna type has the advantage because it becomes a knot.

Since these and the knotted pile are of the same family, they are made in the same manner and you are referred to that section for all details except the construction of the pile. That does differ, and requires further elaboration.

A smooth, flat stick is needed to pick up the pile into loops with this system. Flat metal rods or wooden dowels can also be used, though you may find the dowel too fat for comfortable use in anything but a low pile. These can be bought in various heights from any lumber yard or metal supply place. The girth of the stick determines the height of the pile. The pile guide used in knotting pile can serve this purpose quite adequately and the slit can be used for cutting the loop if the pile is to be cut. When using the Sehna loop, or the Ghiordes, the stick seems to work better if one of its ends is whittled into a hook.

PICK-INSERTED LOOP

To form the pile, insert pile yarn in a plain weave shed as you would a pick of filling. With the shed still open, and beginning on the side of the rug into which the pick was inserted so that yarn can feed freely from the shuttle, pick up yarn between the warp ends, and loop onto a stick equivalent in height to the height of pile desired. (The pile loop does not have to come from between every warp end that is up—it can come from between every 2 or more.) Close the

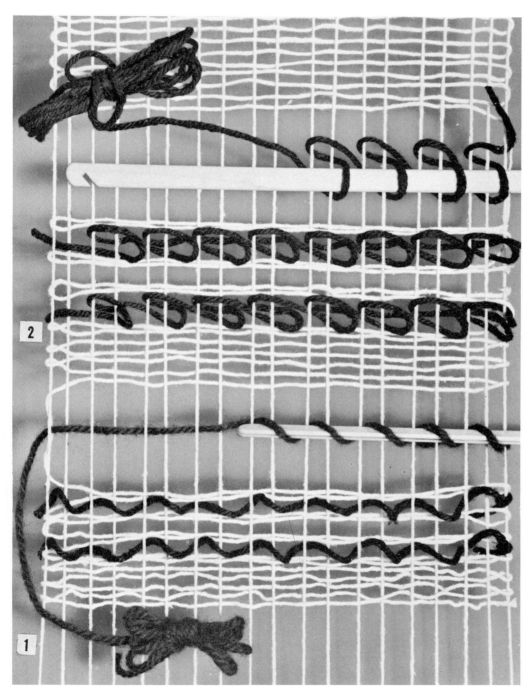

FIG. 67. (*1*) Pick-inserted pile loop. *First 2 rows:* Pile after the pick-up stick has been removed. *Third row:* Pile being picked up with the stick. (*2*) Sehna loop, yarn picked up from the surface of the rug. *First 2 rows:* Pile after the stick has been removed. *Third row:* Pile being picked up with stick.

79

shed; insert regular non-pile filling; beat; and pull out the stick. Change the shed and beat hard again. The stick may be left in if you wish while more than one pick is inserted, but the beat seems to close up the pile pick better after just one pick of filling has been inserted. Insert the rest of the picks of regular filling; and continue alternating pile picks with regular filling until the rug is finished. Bubbling the filling will make for a firmer rug. The number of filling picks between pile rows, just as in the knotted pile, depends upon the height of the loop, the number of strands in the pile, and the density of pile desired. The pile yarn should be pulled up around the stick just tightly enough so there is no slack, otherwise the loops will not be of uniform height.

If more than one color appears in the design in the same horizontal row of pile, a pick of each color is inserted in the same shed, and the loops are pulled up from each according to the area in the row where each color appears. Obviously, a design using this pile system should not be planned with too many color areas in a row or the pile pick will be too fat for good construction. One could get around this and still get much the same effect by separating the row of pile into 2 sheds with a pick of fine but strong filling between. Or—by inserting each different pile yarn as filling within the area of the row in which its loops appear. The first and last loops, in the latter case, would be almost sure to pull out unless the ends of each portion of the pick, separately inserted, are pulled to the surface of the rug and trimmed to the height of the pile.

The pile yarn can be looped in every row of pile in exactly the same position each time, so that one loop is directly above the other throughout the rug; or it can be looped so that its position is varied throughout the rug. Which of these one would want to use at a given time would depend upon the design of that

particular rug; the varied position of the loop might add activity to a rug which already has enough. To have the loop coming from the same position throughout the rug, the pick of pile is always inserted in the same shed of plain weave and all loops are made between the same warp ends. For instance, if the first row of pile were inserted in the shed with even ends up and the loops made between every warp end, all further pile rows would be made while the even ends are up and the yarn is looped between every warp end. If started with odd ends up and loops made between every 2 warp ends up, all further pile rows would be made with the odd ends up and the yarn looped between every 2 warp ends. The sequence of plain weave should not be interrupted if the maximum degree of firmness is desired. With this sequence of pile looping, therefore, the filling picks between the rows of pile will have to be uneven in number.

Varying the position of the pile loop can result in interesting textural effects. This can be done in a number of ways, including: (a) inserting pile yarn in the same pick but having the loops come up between a different number of warp ends, either in the same or separate rows; and (b) inserting pile yarn in alternating picks of the plain weave and having the loops come up between the same number of warp ends. Using a shed other than plain weave for the pile row, such as the 2 up, 2 down of the basket weave or the 2 up, 2 down of the even-sided twill, is another way of varying the loop's position as well as giving it a wider look. The loops in this system are a little more prone to pulling out, but dense pile or latexing the back could avert this. Regardless of the sheds used for pile filling, the weaving between pile rows should continue to be plain weave because its closer interlacing holds the pile more firmly in place.

The pile in rugs of this type can vary from a fine low loop to a heavy or many-stranded high loop. If the texture is to be fine and low, the warp yarn could be of small size such as 6- or 8-ply cotton cord or their equivalents spaced about 12 to the inch; if heavier, the warp can be coarser—10- or 12-ply cotton cord spaced about 8 to the inch. These should not be considered absolute "yardsticks"—they are merely guides from which to begin. The flexibility of a rug warp is quite dependent upon how the filling is treated, and this is best determined by experimenting with sample warps. For instance, the just mentioned finer warp with more ends to the inch could also be used for the coarser textured loop or for a combination of heavy and fine loops, by skipping more ends between loops in the coarser textured areas. Conversely, the heavier warp could be used for fine textures, or a combination of heavy and fine, by having the fine loops come up—not from a pick of filling and between every other end—but from underneath the rug and between every end. In essence, this "underneath" system of feeding yarn is closely akin to the hooked rug method but it is done while, rather than after, the foundation fabric is being woven.

Many rugs made with this system outline motifs of the design with flat areas. This is done by pulling up loops only in the pile areas and leaving the pile in the flat areas to appear as picks of filling. When beginning to loop again after the gap of a flat weave area, one must be careful to leave enough slack in the pile yarn so that warp ends do not pull together, or the loops next to the flat weave areas will be lower than the others.

SEHNA LOOP

This loop is made when the shed is closed and with the pile yarn coming from on top of the warp. Just like the Sehna knot, it too can be made in both directions. The pile yarn should be feeding from the left when working from the right-hand side of the rug, and from the right when working from the left-hand side of the rug. Working from the right-

FIG. 68. Details of the rug shown in Fig. 14. Pick-inserted pile. (Courtesy of The Hispanic Society of America.)

81

FIG. 69. Details of the rug shown in Fig. 14. Pick-inserted pile. (Courtesy of The Hispanic Society of America.)

hand side of the rug, hold the stick in your right hand; insert it under the second and third ends and pull the end of the pile yarn through to the surface to begin pile. Insert the stick under the next 2 ends (4th and 5th) and pull the yarn into a loop onto the stick; continue pulling loops from under two successive warp ends until the row is finished, changing the source of yarn when the design so requires. These directions apply in reverse, of course, when loops are made from left to right. The loops can be made closer by pulling a loop from under every

warp end; and farther apart by pulling a loop from under more than 2 warp ends.

Most of the effects which are possible with knotted pile can also be achieved with this method.

WARP PILE LOOPS

This is a type of pile which can be woven on a handloom with 2 warp beams and 4 harnesses, but which is much more frequently left to the manufacturer. Two warps are necessary—one for the foundation fabric, the other for the pile. The

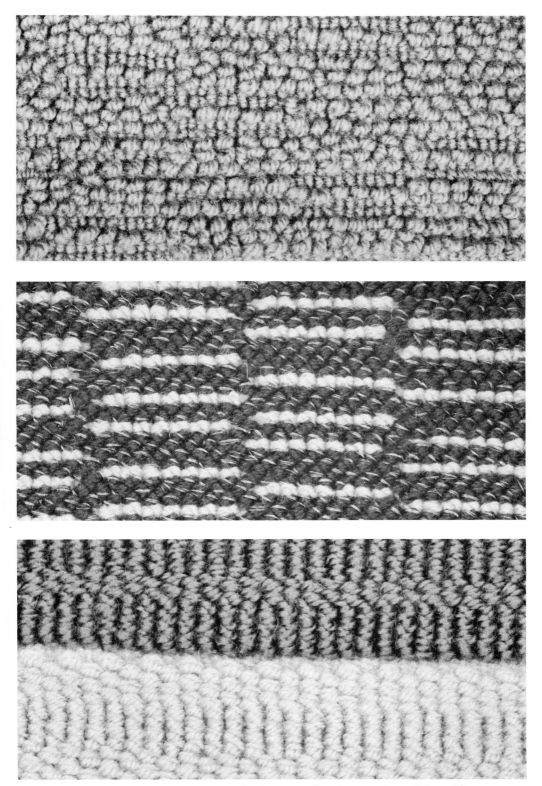

FIGS. 70A, B, & C. Examples of pick-inserted pile. From various pick positions.

loops are made and held in place by raising the pile warp over rods the height of the pile desired. Both warps are then woven together in plain weave with enough tight picks in between the loops to hold them in place. The pile can either be cut or left uncut. The rods used by manufacturers are equipped with ends that automatically cut the loops as they are pulled out; the handweaver can cut them with scissors when the rug is off the loom. It is best to leave a series of these rods in place before removing them gradually and re-using them as the rug progresses.

Each warp has to have its separate warp beam because the loops of the pile warp take up so much yarn so much faster than the foundation warp; for this reason, too, the pile warp will have to be much longer than the foundation warp.

Because each warp works separately, each warp has to be drawn on its own set of harnesses and each must use at least 2 harnesses to produce the simplest weave. The ratio of foundation warp ends to pile warp ends depends upon density of pile. It may be 1 to 1, or 2 foundation to 1 pile, or even stripes of pile alternating with stripes of no pile. But the foundation fabric must be firm and closely woven or the loops will pull out, and the rug will be flimsy. Assuming the ratio to be 2 foundation to 1 pile warp ends, and that the first 2 harnesses were for the foundation warp and the last 2 harnesses for the pile warp, one repeat of the drawing-in of the ends would be: foundation end in harness 1, foundation end in harness 2, pile end in harness 3, foundation end in harness 1, foundation end in harness 2, pile end in harness 4.

Although the color and yarn texture of the loops is fixed by the pile warp, other variations in effect can occur through treatment of the rug in a horizontal direction. The effects need not all be achieved through pile, they can be a combination of pile and non-pile, with the pile warp weaving together with the foundation warp. (See Warp Floats, page 89, for further possibilities.)

CHAPTER 8

Floated Pile Rugs

FILLING FLOATS

This is probably the fastest method of forming pile because, unlike the other systems so far described, the pile yarn needs no manipulation into knots or loops —it is inserted as any filling would be in a flat fabric weave, which this is. Although it has its limitations, and lacks the versatility of the other pile systems, it can be used to make interesting and attractive rugs.

It is made in such a way that each pick of filling which forms the pile is interlaced with the warp at certain intervals within the pick and allowed to float over the warp between those intervals. This eventually forms vertical rows of filling floats which when cut—usually in the center—form the substance of the pile. Since the warp under the float of the pile pick is not in any way interlaced, picks of plain weave are needed between pile rows, not so much to hold the pile in place because the pile does interlace at points between floats, but to incorporate it into a fabric.

Because of the floats in this type of rug, only certain warp ends interlace with the pile picks. To do this, they must be isolated from all other warp ends which interlace differently by being drawn into their own separate harnesses. Since the simplest interlacing requires at least 2 harnesses, these warp ends will then need

2, while the other warp ends which interlace only with the plain weave picks will need 2, a total of 4 harnesses. The distribution of warp ends in the various harnesses depends upon (a) the width of interlacing between floats; and (b) the length of the floats. If many warp ends are interlaced with pile picks between floats it merely changes the design character of the rug; but if too few are used, the pile tufts would be prone to pull out. The interlacing of less than 4 under normal warp and filling conditions is a bit risky.

Two things must be remembered when planning the length of the float. The pile will be only half as long as each float if that float is cut in the center, which it normally is, though off-center cutting for design purposes is legitimate unless it increases the possibility of the tufts pulling out; and the expanse of plain weave exposable to view will be almost as wide as the floats were before they were cut, although thickness of pile can alter this somewhat. Pile can vary in length even in the same rug by having some of the vertical rows made up of long floats, and others made up of short floats.

Unless the warp yarn is firm and heavy, this kind of rug can be rather flimsy; 10- or 12-ply cotton cord or their equivalents

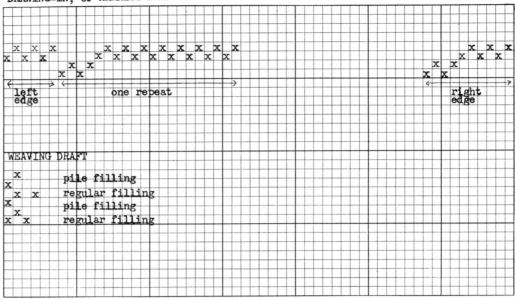

FIG. 71

are good weights and usually work well when spaced 8 to the inch. If heavier filling is used for the plain weave picks, 8-ply cotton cord set 8 to the inch can also make a firm rug. The pile picks can be made up of one or more strands of medium-sized wool, linen, or other decorative type yarn, or of many strands. Multiple-strand pile picks will make a denser pile, but may also cause the rug to build up more quickly in the areas where the pile picks are interlaced. If this happens, extra picks can be woven now and then, only in the areas of plain weave, until those areas are built up to correspond to the pile picks.

Medium-size yarn equivalent to 10- or 12-ply cotton cord can be used for the regular filling or plain weave picks. Because of the nature of this weave, some

FIG. 72. A sample made with the weave shown in Fig. 71. Three strands of yarn per pick.

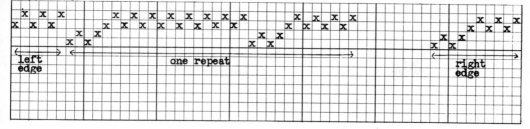

FIG. 73

of the foundation fabric usually shows. It is therefore advisable to consider using either the same kind of decorative yarn as the pile, or yarn much in the same color tones as the pile. While theoretically it is not necessary, bubbling the yarn of the plain weave picks does hold the pile tufts in more securely.

The accompanying drafts are for typical use of this system in all-over pile rugs. They are to be read from the bottom up, with the assumption that the warp is drawn in from the back to the front of the loom. The warp yarn is assumed to be 12-ply cotton cord spaced 8 ends to the inch, 4 ends interlacing with the pile picks. Harnesses 1 and 2 are used for

warp ends interlacing with the pile picks, and all other harnesses for all other ends. Because tufts of pile would look wispy beyond the edge of the rug unless there were some plain weave under it, the drawing-in drafts take into account that there ought to be an edge of about ¾ inch of plain weave on both sides of a rug with a 1-inch long pile. When inserting pile picks, the yarn can stick out beyond the edge, later to be trimmed slightly beyond edge of the rug.

The floats in Figs. 71 and 74 are a uniform length of 2 inches. Any variation in length or in spacing of floats would, of course, alter the single pattern repeat which in that of Fig. 71 is on 20 ends—

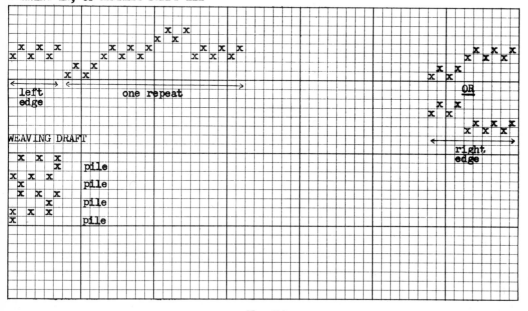

FIG. 74

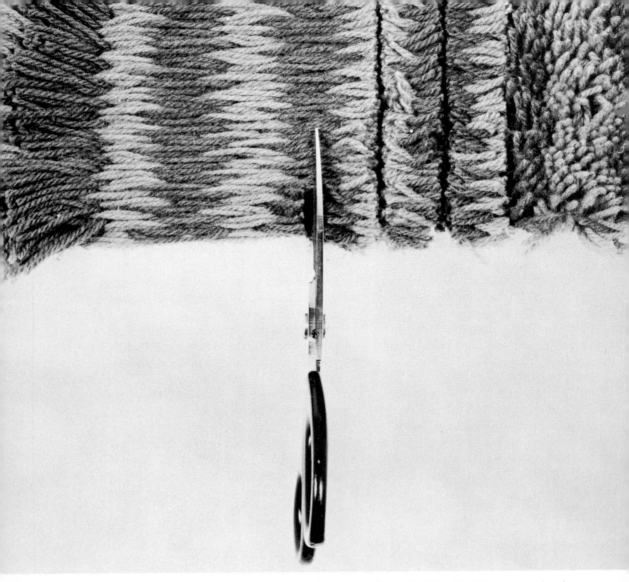

FIG. 75. All-pile sample made with the weave shown in Fig. 74. Three strands of yarn per pile pick, one color pick alternating with another color pick. From left to right, sample shows (*a*) floats uncut; (*b*) floats being cut; (*c*) floats cut but not separated; and (*d*) floats cut and separated.

4 ends for pile interlacing and 16 for plain weave interlacing (8 ends per inch x 2-inch long floats).

The preceding drawing-in draft of Fig. 73 shows, for instance, how the pattern for a rug with vertical rows of 2-inch long floats alternating with 1-inch long floats repeats on 32 ends. The weaving draft is the same as the previous one.

For those weavers with more than a 4-harness-loom capacity, it is possible to cut down the stripiness of this type of all-pile rug by alternating the interlacings

of each pile row so that the floats in each succeeding pile row cover the interlacings of the previous one. This also increases the possibilities of variations in design. The drafts shown in Fig. 74 show how this can be done on 6 harnesses.

HEMS. Like most other rugs, hems should be woven at either end of this type, and later finished in any of the ways described under "Finishing the Woven Rug," page 50.

CUTTING THE PILE. In the 4-harness rug, the pile is cut by running scissors

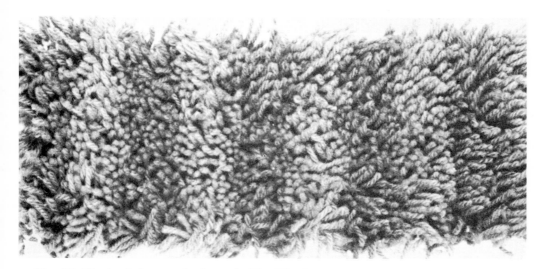

FIG. 76. Floats of the sample shown in Fig. 75, all cut and separated. Alternating colors of pile result in vertical stripes.

along the center of each vertical row of floats, and the tufts are then brushed up to fluff them up. In the 6-harness variety, the floats are cut in the same way but, because the floats overlap, one must be careful to cut each row directly above the pile pick interlacings to be sure that floats from adjacent rows are not inadvertently cut. After cutting, the floats remain overlapped unless taken apart by running a finger or end of a pencil or skewer to separate them and fluff them into upstanding pile.

DESIGN VARIATIONS. Any number of different effects can be produced with this pile system by such devices as:

1. Varying the spacing of pile floats.
2. Varying the length of floats.
3. Varying the number of warp ends interlacing with the picks between floats.
4. Imaginative use of color, either in single picks or overall.
5. Combining plain with pile areas.
6. Checkerboarding the pile in the 6-harness type.

FIG. 77. Detail of a sisal rug with floated pile, cut and trimmed. Woven in Taiwan on a tatami loom. Taiwanese photograph. (Courtesy of *Handweaver and Craftsman* magazine.)

WARP FLOATS

The same type of technique as the filling float pile can be used in reverse. Actually, this is the same system as the Warp Pile Loop, page 82. Two warp beams, 2 warps, and at least 4 harnesses (2 for each of the warps) are required. The only difference is that instead of being raised into loops over rods, the pile warp is left floating on the surface of the fabric for the number of inches required to make the length of pile desired, and then woven in securely with the foundation for a few picks to hold the floats in place. To keep the pile floating while the foundation fabric is being woven, the pile harnesses are kept raised all the time.

The rows of floats are formed in a horizontal rather than a vertical position and are therefore cut with scissors after the rug is finished from edge to edge rather than from end to end, as they are in the filling floated rug, as we have seen previously.

When a loom with more harnesses is available, the pile warp can be staggered in somewhat the same manner as the filling floated pile. The pile must all be woven proportionately into the foundation, however, or more than 2 warp beams would be required.

CHAPTER 9

The Hooked Rug

The term "hooked" is as much a misnomer for this type of pile rug which is now more often punched than hooked, as is the term "knotted" for the pile rug which is not made with a real knot. Since the eventual results are the same, and no one can tell by looking at the completed product whether a punch needle or a hook has been used, this book will take the liberty of calling either type a "hooked" rug.

Pile in this kind of rug is inserted into an already woven foundation fabric. The pile loops are formed in 1 of 2 ways: by *pushing* or by *pulling* the pile yarn into the foundation. In either method, the side of the foundation fabric on which the design has been drawn faces the maker as he works. In the "pushing," or punching, method this becomes the back of the rug from which a yarn-threaded needle pushes the loops onto the other side, or front of the rug; in the "pulling." or hooking, method this becomes the front of the rug because the yarn is fed by pulling it into loops with a wooden-handled hook from underneath the work onto the top, or front of the rug. In the first method, one can be sure that the loops have been properly inserted from the back, but must turn the work over now and then to see what the rug will look like when finished. In the second method, one can see what the rug will look like as work progresses, but must turn the work over every so often to see if the loops are evenly or properly inserted.

Neither tool is better than the other—very attractive rugs with all sorts of effects can be made with both; but the punch needle is the less exacting, is easier for most people to handle, and is faster. The punch needle is preset to a given height and automatically punches that length loop, whereas the hook is controlled completely by hand and the height and evenness of the pile has to be judged by eye. The eye is soon trained, however, and judgment of pile height usually becomes fairly automatic; the eye does need more frequent adjustment when various heights of pile are used in the same rug.

The range of pile heights with the punch needle is from about $\frac{1}{4}$ inch to about $\frac{7}{8}$ inch so that pile shorter or longer than those might require the use of a hook. There are ways of using the needle, as discussed in a later paragraph, which could modify the use of the needle in this respect. It might be mentioned here that it is possible to use the knotting method described on page 77 in combination with the punch needle instead of the hook in a case of this kind; needless to say, the work would have to be turned over so that knotting could take place on the face of the rug. Yarn works much

FIG. 78. Contemporary hooked rug—low looped pile of jute, and higher cut pile of ramie. Made in Taiwan.

better with the punch needle—the hook is apt to split it. A hook is necessary when strips of fabric are too wide to feed through even the bigger eye of the 2 needles furnished with each punch needle.

Other types of automatic punch needles are available, but they require two hands to manipulate and therefore are not as versatile as the one under discussion.

FOUNDATION FABRIC

This should be a good grade of cloth, evenly and firmly woven with twisted yarns such as warp cloth, duraback, or burlap. Many burlaps now on the market are unevenly woven of weak jute yarn and are not suitable for rug-making purposes. An inferior fabric not only wears badly, it is also hard to work with. A good grade of fabric usually has about 15 vertical and 15 horizontal twisted threads to the square inch. The width of the foundation fabric ideally should be at least the width of the rug plus enough extra for generous hems to be turned under on either side of the rug. If it is not possible to find fabric of that width in your vicinity (it can usually be ordered by mail, however), it can be pieced by overlapping two pieces for about an inch and basting together both edges of the overlap before any work is begun. The length should be equal to the length of the rug, plus enough extra to make generous hems to be turned under on either end of the rug, preferably including a few extra inches for attachment to the frame at both ends. No matter what the shape of the rug, a rectangular piece of fabric must be used, and the foregoing measurements must be applied to the widest and longest dimensions of the rug.

A finished hem of 3 inches is a generous one, which means that the unhooked edge all around the rug would be about $3\frac{1}{2}$ inches, the $\frac{1}{2}$ inch to be turned under to prevent raveling. A narrower hem is permissible, of course, but anything under 2 inches is a bit skimpy and somehow gives not quite as good a finish. While the selvage does not have to be turned under because it cannot ravel, it makes for a better finish if it is turned under and treated in the same manner as the ends where it is necessary to do so.

APPLYING DESIGN

Unless the hooking frame is large enough to stretch the rug to full size,

Fig. 79. A 19th-century American hooked wool rug, with cut and uncut loops. (Courtesy of The Metropolitan Museum of Art, Rogers Fund, 1948.)

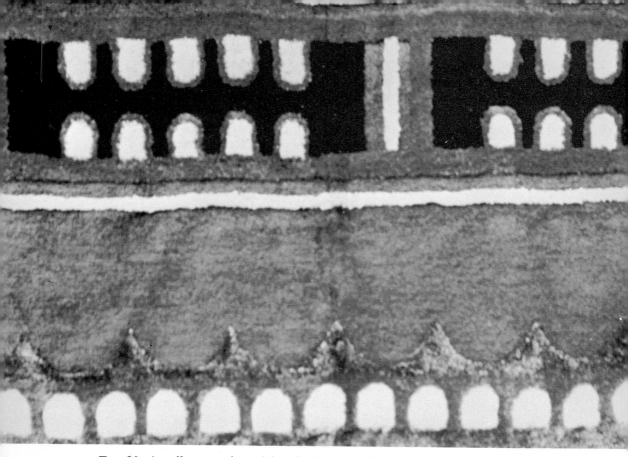

FIG. 80. An all-cut ramie and jute hooked rug. Contemporary Taiwanese, adapted from an aboriginal jacket design. Made and photographed in Taiwan.

the design should be drawn on the foundation fabric before it is stretched onto the hooking frame. Lay the fabric on a flat surface to its full size, thumbtacking it in place so it will remain stationary, making sure that the cloth runs in straight horizontal and vertical lines. Carefully transfer the design to the foundation fabric, being sure that adequate hems are left on all sides of the fabric for turning under when rug is completed. The design, which should first be drawn to full scale on a heavy piece of paper, can be transferred to the foundation cloth in several ways, including (1) tracing with heavy carbon paper; (2) making a stencil of it and tracing with felt-tipped marker; or (3) cutting it out gradually section by section and tracing the design with pen and ink or felt-tipped marker. Whichever method you use, pin or thumbtack securely to the fabric before tracing.

It must be remembered that when a punch needle is used, the design being followed from the back will be in reverse on the front of the rug. In other words, a motif on the left side of the design while being punched will appear on the right of the finished rug; a figure on the right facing left while being punched will appear on the left facing right on the front of the rug. If the design is a symmetrical one this will not matter—both sides will be equal. If not, then the paper design should be turned over before tracing onto the foundation fabric.

THE FRAME

While it is possible to hook a rug on one's lap, it is not comfortable, especially if the rug is more than doormat size. The more the rug progresses, the more cumbersome it becomes. Any method of hooking works at maximum ease and efficiency only when the fabric is stretched taut with the aid of some sort of frame.

This can be one of several types, from a very inexpensive and simple picture frame kind to more elaborate tiltable kinds with floor stands and end pieces which rotate in much the manner that the beams of a loom work. In fact, a loom with the harnesses removed can certainly double as a frame. The better the equipment, of course, the more comfortable it is to work with; so, if many rugs are contemplated, it may be advisable to invest in the kind which is basically an embroidery frame mounted on a stand for ease of operation. One can sit at this type, which has the added feature of being adjustable to a degree of tilt most comfortable to the rug-maker. Some of them are also adjustable in height. The frame without a base, if rested on one's lap and propped up against a table, works quite comfortably; or it can be used on sawhorses.

The frame itself, regardless of underpinning, should consist of 4 pieces of lumber sturdy enough not to warp when tension is applied. Preferably it should be made in such a way that the two crosspieces are rotatable and movable so that the full length of the canvas can be rolled on at once. As the rug progresses, the finished portion can be wound around the lower crosspiece while the fabric is brought forward from the upper crosspiece.

The inside dimensions of the frame, preferably, should be at least a few inches wider on each side than the width of the rug to be hooked, and between 18–20 inches in the other or vertical direction. It is possible to use the horizontal space completely as working or hooking space throughout the hooking of the rug, but less and less of the vertical space as the work progresses because the roll formed by the finished portion of the rug will take up part of that space. For most purposes, however, between 18–20 inches should be adequate for comfortable work-

ing space. The floor frames one buys are usually about 18 inches in the vertical width, and come in horizontal widths of 20, 40, 50, and 60 inches.

The fabric is attached to and centered within the frame, design side up, no matter what instrument is used for making pile. Attach the fabric about ½ inch away from its end onto the upper crosspiece of the frame with thumbtacks spaced every 2 inches or so apart, making sure that it is tacked in a straight line. (Following the same filling thread across and against the edge of the frame will insure straightness.) If the foundation fabric is of a type that is apt to ravel, it would be wise to stitch all around its raw edges by machine before stretching. Roll the fabric over and around the upper crosspiece making sure that it goes on straight until all but about 30 inches or so are rolled on. Attach the other end of the fabric, ½ inch in, with thumbtacks onto the lower crosspiece. Roll the lower crosspiece toward you until the beginning edge of the rug is about ½ inch clear of the frame so there will be enough working space between the frame and the beginning rows of the rug. Continue rolling from upper crosspiece until the fabric is taut. Rolling the upper crosspiece away from you and the lower crosspiece toward you brings them underneath the stretched section of the fabric where they should be. Attaching a piece of muslin to either end of the frame with thumbtacks eliminates the necessity to tack the foundation fabric to the frame each time a rug is made. The foundation fabric is then basted to the end of the muslin and the whole thing rotated as already described.

The sides must now be pulled taut; insert strong common pins every two inches or so lengthwise and into the edges of the fabric; attach a piece of cotton tape to the end of either side of the frame; bring the tape over the frame and around the first common pin, under the frame and around the second common pin, and repeat, going first over, then

FIG. 81. Tensioning foundation fabric horizontally by means of tape. The fabric has already been made vertically taut. This also illustrates how the drawn design faces the maker; and how the foundation fabric is basted with heavy-duty thread to the muslin which is attached to the crosspieces with tacks.

under the frame until both sides are laced taut; secure the tapes to the upper sides of the frame. By going first over and then under the frame instead of around the frame, the tape is freed as soon as the pins are removed, thus simplifying the process of relacing as the work progresses and is moved forward. Lacing kits are available that work on the same principle except that a clip is used instead of a common pin. If the fabric should loosen during the hooking, retighten in the same way. Loose fabric makes it more difficult to work and is apt to make the rug uneven or crooked. Care should be taken to keep the lines of fabric running straight in both directions or it might distort the shape of the rug.

As the rug progresses, loosen the sides, move the fabric forward by unrolling some

of it from the upper crosspiece and rolling the finished portion onto the lower crosspiece. Relace the fabric from the edges as at the beginning. When a stationary frame is used, the tacks have to be removed and retacked each time the canvas is brought forward for further hooking. This will need to be done in a sideways direction, too, if the rug is wider than the frame. This means that the hooked sections will have to be tacked to the frame eventually. Long tacks will need to be used to hold already hooked sections to the frame.

THE PILE

HOW TO USE THE HOOK. Hold the hook as you would a pencil, with thumb and index finger at base of handle. Hold yarn with the index finger and thumb of

96

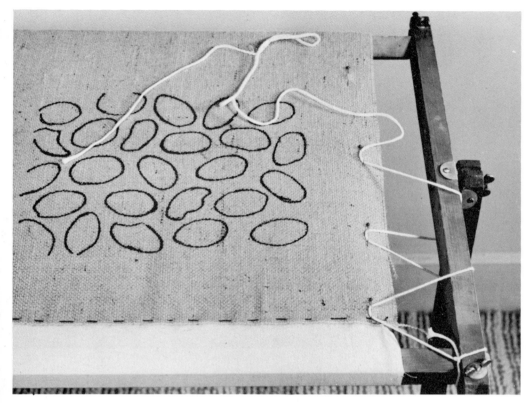

FIG. 82. The path of the tape as it goes over and under the frame and around the pins to tighten the fabric horizontally.

the other hand underneath the fabric. Push the hook into one of the spaces where the threads meet in the fabric and with it pull up the end of the yarn through to the front; insert the hook in the same way one or two spaces away and pull the yarn (still held by thumb and index finger) up to the front with a loop to the height of pile desired. Continue to pull yarn up in the same way into loops until the area with that yarn is finished or until the yarn is used up, whichever happens first, pulling the end of the yarn up to the surface of the rug. You will have to judge the height and evenness of pile by eye, to learn to feed the yarn in such a way that the previous loop is not shortened while pulling up the next loop, and also that the "stitch" on the back connecting one loop to the other is flush with the foundation fabric. All these steps become quite automatic fairly soon—this is not as formi-

dable as it sounds; the fingers soon start making all the necessary adjustments for which it is impossible to give directions.

How to Use the Punch Needle. Insert proper-eyed needle for size of yarn into punch, and fix it to desired height. Thread the yarn first through the eye at the top of the punch and then, from the hollow side, into the eye of the needle. Pulling the yarn up and down a few times while holding it taut at both ends, will ease it into the hollow section of the needle. With the hollow side of the needle facing away from the rug and toward the direction in which the needle is to progress, grasp the handle as you would a pencil. With about an inch of yarn dangling from eye of the needle, insert and punch the needle in the space where threads meet in the fabric. Hold the end of the yarn with your other hand underneath the fabric, pull the needle

97

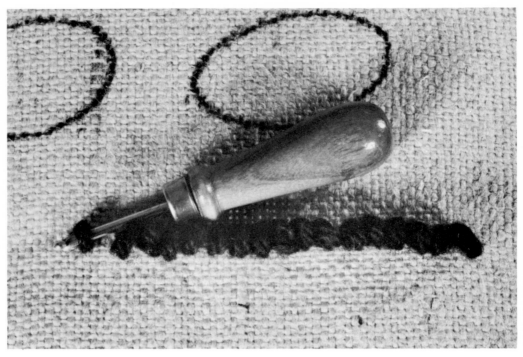

FIG. 83. Hook pulling the loop to the rug's surface from the yarn's source underneath the foundation fabric.

back up just to the surface of the fabric and, keeping needle as close to the fabric as possible, insert it again a space or two away into the fabric as far as the needle will go.

Continue this procedure, making sure that (1) the needle is inserted as far as it will go because the loop is only half as long as the length of yarn pushed in— its principle is that yarn feeds into the needle only when it is being pushed, therefore having to take with it half of the pushed yarn when the needle is being pulled to the surface of the fabric; and (2) that the needle while traveling from loop to loop skims the surface of the fabric; if it is pulled up away from it, it will also carry part of the last inserted loop with it, thereby making it shorter than it should be. If this should happen, pull the yarn of the loop back up, pushing the needle down to meet it at the surface of the fabric, and start again.

All this becomes quite automatic within a very short time. The yarn is held from underneath the fabric only to get the beginning of each strand on the surface of the rug (actually it could as easily be pushed to the surface later). Holding the yarn after that would interfere with the automatic feature of the punch needle and tend to make the loop longer than it should be. If the loop needs assistance from the other hand, it is because the yarn is either too fat or too thin for the particular eyed needle being used; that the yarn has slipped out of the groove of the needle shaft; or that the foundation fabric is too loosely woven.

One can purposely violate the principle of the needle to get the results one wants, however. For those who prefer the needle to the hook but want a higher pile than the $\frac{7}{8}$ inch or so maximum automatically produced by the needle, fix the needle to a length from eye to bottom of handle

98

which is equivalent to the desired height of the pile; punch it into the fabric as far as it will go; with hand underneath the fabric, pick the yarn from eye of needle and hold it in place, thus forcing the yarn to keep feeding through the needle while it is coming back to the surface; the height of pile then will be equal to that punched into the fabric. It can be made shorter than its lowest automatic pile height by inserting a rubber or felt washer below the handle of the needle.

Keep enough loose yarn on top of the work for it to feed freely into the needle, otherwise the loops will be either shorter than they should be or miss completely.

Gently holding the already formed pile aside with a hand underneath the fabric in the area where pile is being punched will prevent the needle from getting caught into it and possibly pulling out some of the loops. For the same reason, it is suggested that the low pile areas be punched in after the high pile.

Thin yarns can be used as well as rather thick ones. A yarn can be used singly in the punch needle or in multiple strands. The needle itself controls the number of strands which can be used. There must be just a slight amount of tension for the needle to work at its best.

DENSITY OF PILE

This is determined by the size of the yarn, the height of pile, and by the number of threads skipped on the foundation

FIG. 84. Pushing yarn with a punch needle from the back of the rug to form loops on the rug's surface, underneath the foundation fabric.

FIG. 85. Backs of hooked rug samples, showing various directions in which the punch needle can be made to go.

fabric between the loops of pile. The loops should be spaced close enough to give the rug a firm, solid feel. If the loops are too far apart, the rug will look a little tired and will not wear well; if they are overcrowded it will be boardlike and not hug the floor too well. To find the happy medium, try out a few square inches before beginning the rug. Loops will require closer spacing with fine yarn than with heavy yarn, and with low pile than with high pile.

EFFECTS WITH PILE

The needle or hook can be manipulated so that the pile goes in straight lines, in swirls, follows pattern outlines, zigzags, or in any other way you wish it to go. If the pile is cut, the direction in which it was hooked doesn't show, so the straight line method is easiest and fastest; if the pile is looped, the direction does show, the lower the pile the more so. The straight-row method of hooking gives a more angular look; the swirl adds to the textural effect which in some cases can be more interesting than the angularity of the straight-line hooking; when using yarn or cloth from different dye lots, this is a good method of blending them. Which of any of these you use should depend upon the design. If the design already has much activity, you may want to minimize the direction of the work; or you may want to accent or emphasize certain contours of the design and work around or in the same direction as those contours.

The pile can be all cut, all looped, or a combination of cut and looped. Cut pile has a more velvety appearance, and is deeper and more intense in hue than uncut pile of the same color and yarn. When the two are used in combination, the textural and shading effects can be quite striking. When cutting pile, insert one blade of the scissors into as many loops as you can, gently pulling the blade up to the full height of the loop. It is easier and faster to pick up and cut many loops at one time with the scissors if hooking is done in straight lines and cutting is done after each line is completed, rather than when several lines have accumulated. The tops of the loops can be cut off instead if you prefer, but it should be taken into account when making the loop that this will shorten the pile.

The height of pile in a single rug can either be uniform or of several heights. It can vary in effect from a very fine low loop that almost reminds one of needlepoint to a heavy, high pile with a shaggy look, and all the variations in between, cut and uncut.

A very low row of pile which does not show is a good device to hold the pile up to some extent, yet let it fall as though there were open spaces between rows of piled areas. This can also be achieved by leaving unhooked gaps in the fabric; in this case pile should be long or dense enough so that the fabric cannot ever be exposed to view. This is also one way to get a sculptured look without cutting.

If the proper yarns are used, practically all the effects described in the Knotted Rug section of Chapter 3 can be simulated with hooking to produce rugs that can rival the handknotted types. Not that any craft should be embarrassed with itself —but, what is a hooked rug, after all? Primarily a pile rug; and any pile effect that can be exploited with the medium is fair and legitimate. In fact, as already mentioned, the two types can sometimes be combined to advantage, particularly where long, shaggy pile comes into play.

BACKING

While it is not absolutely necessary to cover the back of a rug with some sort of adhesive it is advisable to do so for two reasons. It anchors the loops into place and prevents them from pulling out; and it makes the rug skidproof. This latter is important particularly in small rugs.

This rug adhesive can be purchased

101

Fig. 86. Face of the sample shown at the right of Fig. 85. Two heights of cut pile. Spaces left unhooked allow the long pile to fall into flowerlike formations.

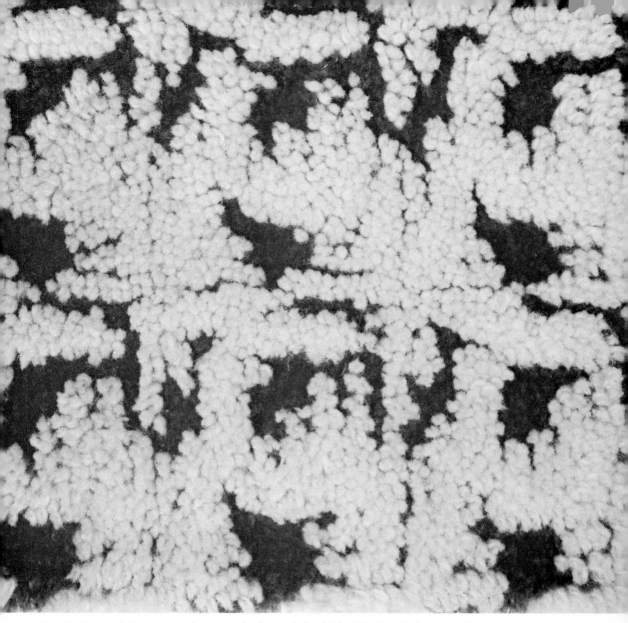

FIG. 87. Face of the sample shown at the lower left of Fig. 85. Two heights of all-cut pile.

in many department or hardware stores or mail order firms. It can be painted on with a paintbrush. The whole rug ought to be laid out, face down, on a flat surface, taking care that it is even; otherwise the adhesive will make the rug uneven. Once the adhesive is on, it stiffens in place. If the rug can be stretched all at once on the frame on which it was made, apply adhesive while still stretched.

HEMMING

To finish the edges, turn the rug upside down and evenly trim all around. Turn the hem close enough to the edge of pile so the canvas does not show, but not so close that edge-row of pile will gap open and show canvas on the surface of the rug; turn in the raw edge about ½ inch and pin to rug. Miter the corners of an angular-cornered rug, cutting away any excess which might make the corners lumpy. Ease in the hem of a circular or oval rug. You may have to put in a small pleat now and then, but easing usually makes it possible to fit the excess caused by the curve being smaller at the hemming point. A flatter, smoother surface can be achieved by placing pins at close intervals rather than by placing pins far apart between humps of fabric. After the hem is pinned, either all around or in sections, sew through the foundation with a blind hemstitch with carpet or heavy duty cotton thread.

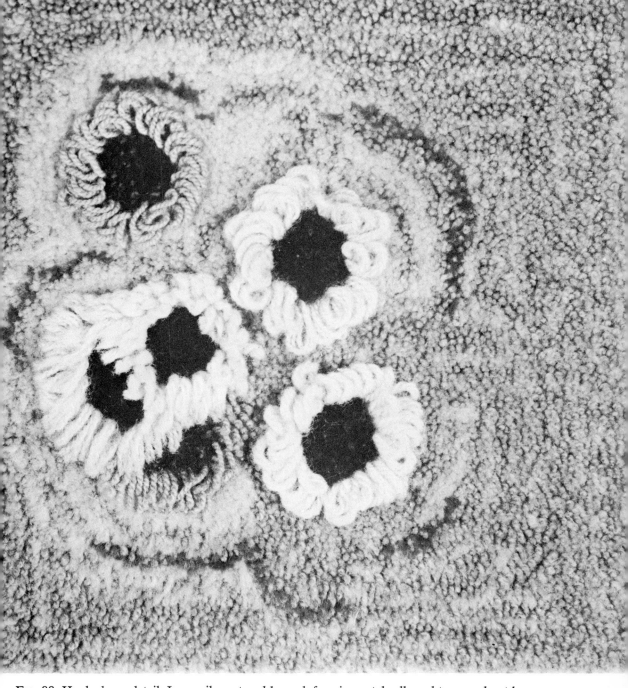

FIG. 88. Hooked rug detail. Long pile, cut and looped, forming petals allowed to spread out by leaving sections of the canvas unhooked.

FIG. 89. Early 19th-century New England hooked rug. (Courtesy of The Metropolitan Museum of Art, Rogers Fund, 1918.)

FLAT RUGS

Ever since man in prehistory discovered the process of interlacing pieces of grass with other pieces of grass, we have had the potential for weaving flat rugs and carpets. And every new weave and some of its variations developed since then has increased that potential, because rugs differ from other types of fabrics only in that they are destined for the floor. Obviously, a piece of cotton sheeting, even though nailed to the floor, would not last long enough to become anything but a rag in a short time. But, let that same plain weave be used with heavier warp and filling yarns and its character changes. It becomes sturdier, holds the floor better, and therefore becomes more suitable as a floor covering. The same can be said of most of the other weaves and some of their variations, provided they are properly adapted to the role a rug plays.

Many types of weaves which have become associated in people's minds as rug types started out as blankets which eventually progressed in degree of luxury to the floor. Actually, blankets and rugs were often interchangeable in the past and probably still are in certain world areas. Yarns and colors available had much to do with the popularity of some of those weaves which certain eras accepted as current style.

Depending upon what kind of yarns and looms are available for your use, any one of the weaves could conceivably at some point be used for a rug. Spongy types of heavy yarns like handspun wool or cotton roving, which are quite beautiful in themselves, can be most attractive woven in a single color plain weave, with probably a heavy fringe to dramatize the simplicity of the whole. Sisal, heavy linen, or jute if a heavy enough loom is available can be used quite effectively in certain types of weaves which are more often used for decorative fabrics or clothing. Twills, herringbones, and diamond patterns can come out of the category of strong diagonals which might be too blatant for contemporary floor use, if outlined with long pile, or if made in colors that rather subtly blend into one another; or which, in reverse, purposely emphasize the diagonal with the use of heavy yarns that cover the filling or the warp. The list of rug possibilities in the use of all types of flat weaves is too long to enable us to study more than a few types that have proved consistently successful as floor coverings.

The flat weaves that have been most often successful as rugs are the type in which the pattern yarn covers the other set of yarn. The pattern yarn can run either in the direction of the warp, with the filling completely covered; or, as is more frequently the case in handloomed rugs, it can run in the direction of the filling, with the warp completely covered. It is easy to understand why this system of close interlacing is so often employed for rugs—it allows one set of yarn to be so closely packed in that the fabric becomes firm and heavy, a suitable quality. The earliest use of a weave in this manner for a rug was the tapestry rug.

FIG. 90. Ramie rug sample. Flat weave done on herringbone threading, long, shaggy Ghiordes-knotted pile outlining the weave. Woven and photographed in Taiwan.

CHAPTER 10

The Tapestry Rug

This type of weave comes to us from probably as far back as the Stone or Bronze Age. Since all primitive peoples used it, most archaeologists feel that it arose in each area independently of any influence from outside sources. Exactly when tapestries moved from the bed or wall to replace grass and felted mats as floor coverings is a matter for conjecture, but it was long before the Christian era. It was not a matter of forsaking the walls in favor of floors, however, because the tapestry technique has been and is being used for walls to a much greater extent than for floors. And it is still being used for blankets or bed coverings in some areas of the world. The widespread use of this Old World technique spilled into the New World, acquiring along the years in both worlds such names as "kilims" from the Near East; Peruvian; Navajo; Aubussons and Gobelins from France; and Mexican. While variations occurred in use of the technique, and in each area the tapestry rug took on a character of its own, the basic weave has remained the same. Although many of the old tapestries used as rugs are quite fine, in the main the tapestry rug is heavier and of much simpler design than the wall type.

THE WEAVE

The tapestry weave is nothing more than a plain weave in which all the warp ends are covered. A tapestry rug can run the gamut of complexity from a single-color, one-shuttle rug to a rug with many motifs and color changes and a number of shuttles or bobbins. In a single-color, or a horizontally striped rug, the shuttle can be shot from edge to edge without interruption exactly as it would be in any ordinary plain weave, with the exception that the filling yarn must be fed into the shed just loosely enough so that no warp ends show. But, the tapestry rug is more generally characterized by motifs which break up the horizontal line into color or texture areas. This means that the single shuttle must be replaced by as many shuttles or bobbins per horizontal line, or pick, as there are color or texture changes within that pick. This in no way changes the plain weave; it just requires more sources of yarn to complete each pick in the areas where motifs exist, each source of yarn working back and forth in plain weave, but completing only that part of each pick which falls within the contours of its motif. This creates separate pattern areas which work more or less independently of one another, making it possible to weave tapestry rugs area by area, as well as row by row. But, it also causes certain types of separations in the weaving where motif meets motif which, for reasons of wearing quality or safety, may require slight adjustments in weaving.

FIG. 91. Navajo tapestry wool blanket. (Photograph courtesy of Museum of the American Indian.)

FIG. 92. Tapestry weave—vertical stripes.

Before going into the methods of treating the separations where motif meets motif, or texture meets texture, let us take a few characteristic shapes and follow them through from beginning to end to see what naturally occurs when a tapestry rug is begin woven horizontal row by horizontal row. Although each of these is merely a sample of shapes, and not a complete rug design, use will be made of them to point out simultaneously the steps necessary to make a tapestry rug.

The warp is first prepared and drawn into the loom for a plain weave. It is then stabilized by weaving in sticks and/or heavy yarn, as you would for any other type of fabric. Ending up the preliminary weaving with ½ inch or so of tapestry weave more firmly establishes the rug to its full width. The only difference between this ½ inch and the rest of the preliminary weaving is that it covers the warp ends completely. This is done by opening the shed, shooting the yarn through at an upward diagonal and pushing it down with the fingers toward the weaving a few times across the width of the rug. This forms a series of bubbles or scallops which insure the slack necessary to cover all warp ends. (Bubbling as described under the Knotted Pile section, page 47, is the same except that in the case of the tapestry rug, the warp is usually set farther apart and the bubbles do not usually need to be made so closely to cover the warp.) The shed is then closed and the pick beaten. The actual rug is then begun, using the same method of covering all warp ends as just described, with the exception that each shuttle or bobbin weaves only across its own area of motif.

As in the case of knotted pile rugs, the design at this point can either be painted or inked onto the warp. If a vertical loom is used, the design or cartoon can be placed behind the warp; if a horizontal

111

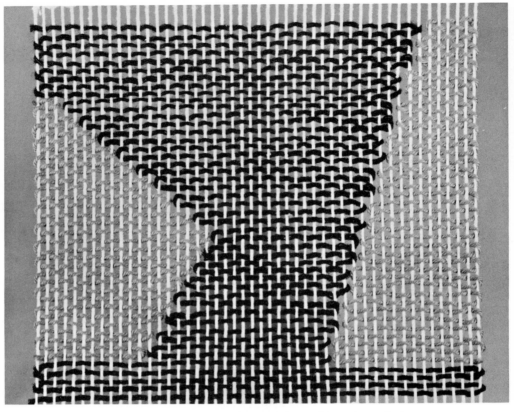

FIG. 93. Tapestry weave—diagonal lines with various pitches.

loom is being used with a hand rather than with its regular beater, the cartoon can be followed by placing it underneath the warp. In either case, there should be enough space between the warp and the cartoon to allow for handling warp comfortably.

The Vertical Stripe (Fig. 92)

Open the shed, insert the first yarn from the left through to the beginning of other color or texture; insert second yarn from its right-hand contour up to the point where it meets the first yarn; close shed and beat. Although in this case it does not matter whether the 2 adjacent yarns come from opposite directions to meet each other, or from the same direction and away from each other, it is often advisable for shuttle to meet shuttle because it is easier to follow sharp changes in contours of the design when this is

done. Change the shed and shoot the shuttles or bobbins back to where they started from. Continue this process until the stripe is finished.

The Diagonal Line (Fig. 93)

In this, 3 types of diagonal line have been combined, each with a different pitch. The one with the lowest pitch (upper left) progresses in every 2 picks from one warp end to 2 beyond it, the one with the next steeper pitch (lower left) progresses in every 2 picks from one warp end to the next; the one with the steepest pitch (right side) works with the same ends for 4 picks before progressing onto the next warp end. A lower pitched diagonal would progress 3 or 4 or more ends at a time, and a steeper pitched one would have more picks between progressions from one warp end to the other. The weave itself is exactly as

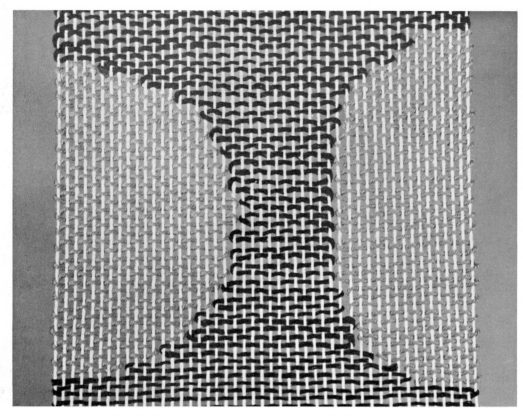

FIG. 94. Tapestry weave—circular and elliptical contours.

in the vertical stripe, but with 3 sets of yarn working instead of 2; the first yarn is inserted from the left, the second from the right, and the third from the left so that all yarns meet and then separate with each successive pick. Since the contours differ, different separations in the weave occur as the illustration shows.

Elliptical & Circular Shapes (Fig. 94)

The illustrations are self-explanatory. Nothing different happens than in the vertical and diagonal lines—it just does the same things in varying degrees.

METHODS OF TREATING SEPARATIONS

A large variety of methods of treating these separations has been used over the years, all of them variations on the same theme. Some can be used only when the back of the work faces the weaver because

they form a ridged seam. Only the simplest and most direct of them will be discussed here, since they are quite adequate for rug-making purposes.

As you can see from the illustrations, a slit naturally occurs in the weaving when color meets color or texture meets texture and continues to do so in a vertical direction, such as in the vertical stripe, the diagonal line with a steep pitch, and the vertical edges of the center of a circular or elliptical line. It can readily be seen from Fig. 92 that something *must* be done for a vertical stripe which runs the full length of a rug or the rug would end up in separate pieces. Otherwise, slits can be very decorative and seem to add an extra dimension which is taken advantage of in most of the loveliest of the kilims from the Near East. If the rug is to be used in an area of a room subject to much traffic, and if you are at all hazard conscious, it might be best to reserve this device for the tapestry not intended as a floor covering. Unless the slits are fairly short they could, in combination with women's high heels, cause tripping. The slits can be sewed on the wrong side later as they are in some wall hangings, but that takes more time than it would take to dovetail or interlock, and it is not apt to be as permanent.

DOVETAILING is the kind of joining in which the yarns adjacent to one another are brought around the same warp end before turning in the other direction to be woven in as the next pick. In one form, sometimes called "comb-toothed," the adjacent yarns weave pick for pick; in another, sometimes called "saw-toothed," one adjacent yarn weaves several picks before the other repeats the same performance. Saw-toothing is faster than comb-toothing because the shuttle does not have to be dropped so often, but it leaves a more pronounced zigzag effect at the juncture of the 2 areas. All dovetailing in a straight vertical line builds the

weaving up at the juncture where 2 adjacent yarns go around one warp end because there is twice as much yarn around that warp end as there is between other warp ends where only one yarn is at work. If the vertical line is short, this presents no problem—it could prove troublesome if the vertical line is a long one such as in a vertically striped rug, in which case you had better use the interlocking device.

Because it is the nature of the plain weave to alternately cover all warp ends with every 2 picks of filling, dovetailing, in one form or another, must automatically occur when other than vertical straight-line sections of motifs are being worked. Since, because of the contour of the outline, it does not always result in the pick-for-pick variety, you may prefer, even when unnecessary, a more definite form of closure, such as "interlocking," which is next described. It is certainly not necessary, but you may prefer to use interlocking even when dovetailing occurs as regularly as it does in the diagonal or circular shapes of the illustrations.

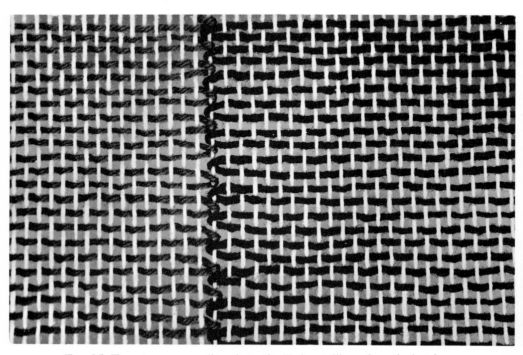

FIG. 95. Tapestry weave—"comb-toothed" dovetailing of vertical stripes.

114

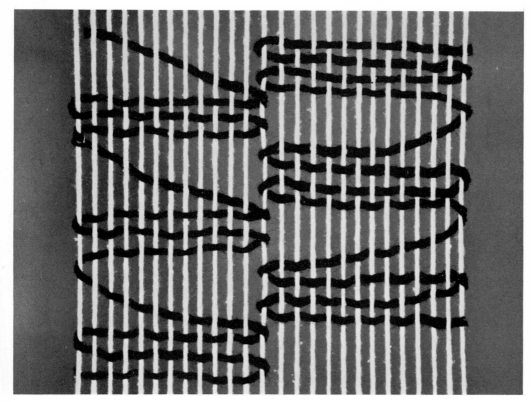

Fig. 96. Tapestry weave—"saw-toothed" dovetailing of vertical stripes.

INTERLOCKING is another method of joining adjacent yarns without forming a slit or dovetailing. In this, the yarns adjacent to one another are linked together between the 2 picks at point of meeting before turning in the other direction to be woven in as the next pick. When the shed is open for receiving the picks after having been linked together, one of these 2 warp ends must be up, the other down. It will be found that a smoother interlocking results if the yarn going through the shed beginning with the up warp end is brought under and over the yarn returning through the shed beginning with the down warp end. The same filling yarn will do this when used in a vertical straight line because the position of the ends is constant, but not so when interlocking is used in other types of contour areas where filling yarns do not weave back and forth from the same spot.

THE LOOM

The tapestry rug can be woven on a horizontal or vertical loom, with or without a beater, and with a 2-shed motion. The loom with a beater is more flexible than one without because the beater can be used in areas where it is necessary or easier and more efficient to build up the rug horizontal row by horizontal row, and can remain unused when it is easier and faster to build up the rug section by section. If or when the beater is not being used, the same kind of small hand beater will be needed which is required when a loom without a beater is used. The kind of metal comb found in pet shops makes a good hand beater. As already stated under caption "The Loom" of the Knotted Pile section, the horizontal loom is more convenient and efficient to work with than the vertical loom. Shuttles and other weaving paraphernalia can find an easy

115

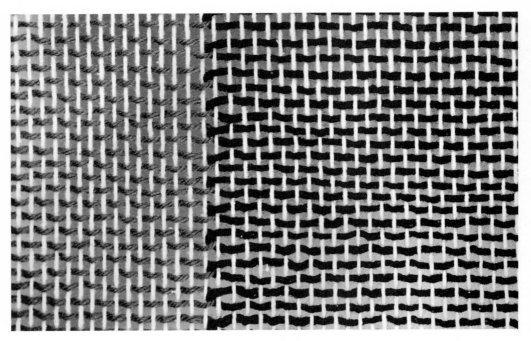

FIG. 97. Tapestry weave—interlocking of vertical stripes.

resting place on top of the finished portion of the rug, and a wider shed can usually be obtained. A vertical loom, on the other hand, takes up less floor space, is often less expensive to buy, and can more easily be made by the home carpenter—sometimes, but not always, at less cost.

Since small details get lost in rugs, and take much more time to do, you may find yourself designing simpler and larger shapes which can be done just as easily row by row as section by section if your loom is the beater type.

Although many tapestries have been woven with the back of the work facing the weaver, it is not at all necessary, and it is much easier to weave with the surface of the rug facing you. Also, tapestries have often been woven with the design on its side, for which there seems to be no sound reason. Could the practice have started after a magnificent and much-admired tapestry, much wider than it was long, was woven on its side because this was the most feasible way to treat the loom situation? A good device, but not

necessary when most rugs are longer than they are wide.

SECTIONAL WEAVING

You will find out readily enough, if you ever weave a tapestry rug section by section, that there are certain types of areas which must be woven at the same time, such as those motifs which you need or prefer to interlock or dovetail with adjacent motifs, and full-width horizontal stripes. You will also find that, although you can sometimes weave whole motifs separately if you so wish, the shapes of other contours dictate that a certain order of sectional weaving take place. In the illustration of diagonal lines (page 112), for instance, looking at it from the bottom up as it would be woven on the loom, the right-hand light-colored section could be completely woven sectionally first; the black could be woven next, but only up to the point where the diagonal of the light-colored left-hand section starts changing direction; the whole of the left-hand light section could be completely

116

Fig. 98. Tapestry weave—interlocking of diagonal lines.

woven next; and last, the rest of the black section. Any other order of sectional weaving would result in a gradual closing in of unwoven areas, making it impossible to insert a shuttle later in those areas to weave them.

WARP AND FILLING

The warp should be spaced far enough apart so that the filling can pack down and cover it without too much trouble. If heavy filling yarn is used, the warp will have to be spaced farther apart than with finer filling. Since a rug of this kind ought to be fairly sturdy in most cases, a heavier, but not too firmly twisted, filling yarn averaging between 500–750 yards per pound is a good weight. With yarn of this size in the filling, 6- or 8-ply cotton cord or its linen or other equivalent can be spaced 6 to the inch to work quite efficiently.

FINISHING THE RUG

The tapestry rug, as is the case with many rugs, can be finished with fringed warp or applied fringe; or with a turned-under hem. The design of the rug dictates the appropriate finish. See Finishing the Woven Rug, page 50, for further details.

FIG. 99. Navajo tapestry wool blanket. (Photograph courtesy of Museum of the American Indian.)

FIG. 100. Striped tapestry rug in greens and blues, flowerlike shapes done with knots lying in 4 directions.

119

FIG. 101. Detail of a plain tapestry weave rug with knotted pile motif. (Photograph by A. Burton Carnes, New York. Courtesy of *Handweaver and Craftsman* magazine.)

CHAPTER 11

The Soumak Rug

This is another of the ancient techniques whose origin is unknown, but which seems to have been in existence since centuries before the Christian era. Beautiful rugs have been and are still being made with it; but it seems to have been used much more extensively in the Near Eastern part of the world and its immediate environs than in the Western world. If one uses it in somewhat the same manner as the Easterners, with fine yarns and fine detail, and with designs much in the style of the kilims (Near Eastern tapestries), it is a time-consuming technique. When used in a more contemporary fashion with heavier yarns, in simpler design form, or in combination with faster-to-make techniques it, like the knotted pile rug, can be made to better conform to the Western time budget. And it can produce most interesting effects!

The soumak resembles the tapestry rug in that it is flat, the warp ends are all covered, and each change of color or texture in a horizontal row requires a separate bobbin. This creates isolated pattern areas, each of which must be worked back and forth with its own yarn. However, it differs from tapestry in that it is not a weave—it is more an embroidery stitch, and its pattern areas cannot be woven in sections. It must be woven horizontal row by horizontal row because it needs strengthening picks of plain weave between soumak rows. Without the weaving, it could conceivably hold together because it is securely wrapped around the warp in such a way that it could not fall apart, but it would be very loose, would curl considerably, and would therefore neither wear nor look well.

THE "STITCH"

It is usually made by bringing a strand of yarn over an even number of warp ends and back under half of those, continuing to progress across the row by going over the original number and back under half again. (The soumak rug has probably not often been made on any number of ends other than 2 or 4, but there seems to be no reason why a larger number could not be used.) As a result, the back of the rug looks like a series of wrapped cords while the front of it looks like a series of diagonally slanted stitches. It is usually made so that one row is worked from left to right and the next from right to left, the slant of the diagonal stitch reversing itself on the return trip, giving it a braidlike or herringbone effect. It is not always used in this manner, the slant is sometimes continued in the same direction.

To make the soumak rug, prepare the warp and set it into the loom for a plain

Fig. 102. Sample of soumak stitch going over 8 and under 4 ends of an 8-ends-to-the-inch warp. The background is done with herringbone effect and the "motif section" with stitch going in the same direction. The black outline when going horizontally is done in regular soumak stitch. When going vertically, it goes over and under 2 ends of its own in each soumak row.

weave. After the warp has been stabilized with preliminary weaving, a hem of some sort—plain, tapestry, or other weave—should be woven in. The length of the hem depends upon how you intend to finish the ends of the rug. See Chapter 4, "Finishing the Woven Rug." The design is either drawn on the warp, or followed from graph paper with each square representing a stitch. See Translating Paper Design into Knots, p. 44, for fuller information.

Now for the first soumak row. Although, as already stated, the stitch can work on any number of warp ends, this will show the repeat over 4, the number most commonly and traditionally used. The yarn can be fed from a bobbin, a butterfly, or whatever is more comfortable for you; any shuttle but a quite small one is cumbersome. The shed is closed when the soumak stitch is being made. Beginning from the extreme left of the rug, tuck yarn in between a few warp ends. Bring yarn over the first 4 warp ends close to the last pick of weaving and backward under 2 warp ends, bringing it to the surface above the loop of the soumak stitch; and repeat across the row, ending with "over 4 ends, backward under

122

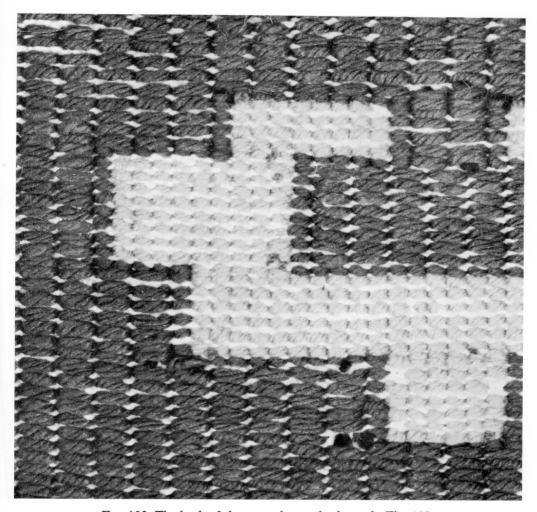

FIG. 103. The back of the soumak sample shown in Fig. 102.

2, and forward over 1, forward under 1." (The latter "forward over 1, forward under 1" are not really part of the stitch —it just seems to the writer a logical way to bring the yarn into position for the next row.) The yarn is now in readiness for its return trip. If more than one color or one yarn are in the same row, the stitch is repeated exactly in the same manner as just described, but only within the confines of its own motif; each new yarn in the same row is treated exactly as is the first yarn. Insert the first pick of the plain weave repeat (odd ends up).

The second row of soumak is worked in reverse, from right to left. Bring yarn from the extreme right of the rug over 4 warp ends close to the last soumak row, backward under 2 ends, bringing it to the surface above the loop of the soumak stitch; and repeat to the end of the row, or motif as the case may be, ending with "over 4 warp ends, backward under 2, and forward over 1, and forward under 1." As in the first row, each pattern area is worked in its own yarn. Insert the second pick of the plain weave repeat (even ends up). Continue following the design, alternating a soumak row with a pick of plain weave until rug is finished.

If the herringbone effect is not wanted, the yarn can either be started from the left-hand side for each row; or the yarn in the second soumak row can be brought over 4 ends, backward under 2, bringing it to the surface from under, instead of over, the loop of the soumak stitch.

In most of the soumaks, the motifs

123

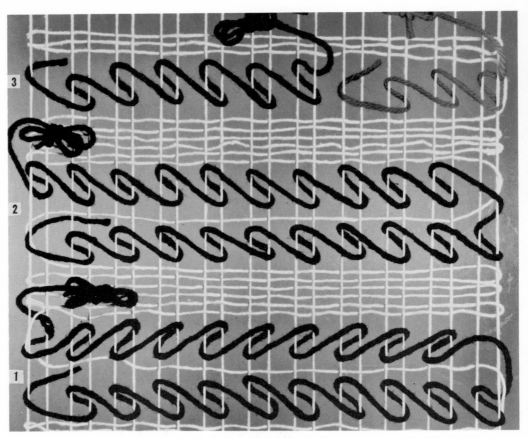

FIG. 104. Soumak stitch. (*1*) Stitch forming a herringbone pattern. (*2*) Stitch lying in the same direction. (*3*) Two colors, or kinds of yarn, in the same row.

are outlined with a contrasting color yarn with a soumak stitch repeating on 2 ends. In the areas where the motif is separated from another in a vertical direction, the warp end at the separation is wrapped round and round with the contrasting color—it is sort of soumak stitch repeating on a single end, upward. The same outlining device is used in many of the Near Eastern kilims.

YARNS

The same type of cotton cord suggested for warp and filling for knotted pile rugs can be used. The soumak pattern yarn can be of wool or any other kind you desire, of a quality commensurate with the time spent in making the rug.

The size of the yarns used for both warp and soumak stitch depends upon the texture one wants. A soumak rug can be fine-textured with fine warp yarn set many ends to the inch, or coarse-textured with heavy warp yarns set few ends to the inch. The setting of the warp determines the number of soumak stitches per inch and, in a sense, the size of the pattern yarn. A many-stitches-to-the-inch texture would suggest a fine soumak yarn; a few-stitches-to-the-inch texture a heavy soumak yarn. An 8-ply cotton cord warp set 12 to the inch would produce 5 stitches per inch when using 4 ends per soumak repeat, 11 stitches using 2 ends per repeat; a 12-ply cotton cord warp set 8 to the inch would produce 3 stitches using 4 ends per soumak repeat, 7 stitches using 2 ends per repeat.

FIG. 105. A jute rug sample. Smaller braid done in soumak stitch with several strands of yarn; bigger braid made by bringing the yarn from underneath the warp and crocheting it onto the surface from between the warp ends. The fringe is Ghiordes knotted. Sample made and photographed in Taiwan.

It is not necessary to alternate one soumak row with one pick of filling. Many rugs alternate 2 soumak rows with one pick of plain weave. Since it takes far less time to insert the filling than it does to make rows of soumak, one would be more tempted to do this in reverse and do only one row of soumak to every 2 or more picks of plain weave. This can be better done in the coarser textured soumak because the heavy yarn covers the filling more easily.

It is possible to make the texture even bolder and thicker by using more than one strand of yarn for the soumak stitch, in which case even more filling can be used between soumak rows. The soumak "weave" can also be used in combination with other techniques such as tapestry or knotted pile. The soumak stitch of the rug illustrated in Fig. 105 is done with many strands of yarn, and is used in combination with an applied braid and long knotted fringe.

CHAPTER 12

Experimental Soumak Rug

With hesitancy the rug of color illustration #3 is put under the classification of a soumak—justifiable strong objections from more orthodox quarters are anticipated—but since it was developed as a result of pondering over the soumak and the possibilities of its deviated use, and since it is more an embroidery stitch than a weave, perhaps it can trail in the soumak wake. Like the soumak, it is similar to the tapestry weave in that each yarn works back and forth within its own area, with the difference that the yarn floats on the surface rather than being interlaced with the warp. Like the soumak, it needs to be strengthened and bound together with picks of plain weave between pattern rows.

Whatever it should be termed, this is the way it was made. Although the method I used to make this rug is given step by step, it is not intended to be a "recipe" for a particular rug but rather a clarification of the principle behind it. The design repeat could just as well have been a series of squares, of diamonds, or flower motifs; the technique can be used in any number of ways to produce any number of pattern variations.

WARP

The design in this case was to repeat on 10 ends, so the warp was made in multiples of 10 ends with 12-ply cotton cord spaced 8 to the inch, drawn into the loom for a plain weave. A finer warp spaced more closely could have been used with a narrowing of the pattern repeat—or with the pattern repeating on more than 10 ends, but I wanted the firmness of the heavier warp as well as the wider stripe. This design was easy to follow without being drawn onto the warp or reading it from graph paper.

FILLING

The same type of yarn as the warp was tried out, but it seemed to have the tendency to show a little—an undesirable effect—so one of the wool yarns of the "stitch," or pattern, was used instead. All filling was bubbled as explained in the Knotted Pile section.

PATTERN YARN

This was made up of 3 strands of 2-ply, firmly twisted wool yarn of about 600 yards to the pound. It could have been made with fewer strands or with finer yarn, but it would have taken more time to build up the rug; or, with only one strand of heavier yarn, but 3 strands spread more than one strand and covered the foundation weaving more readily, at the same time giving it a spongier look.

FIG. 106. Blow-up of the hem, fringe, and stitch of the rug shown in color illustration #3.

The original sample was made with a 4-ply softer twisted yarn which had a fluffier look.

HEMS

Because they were to be turned under and taped to the back of the rug, hems on both ends were made about 1½ inches long with the same yarn as the filling, in the tapestry weave. Though not necessary, had the filling yarn been cotton cord, the hems would still have been woven with one of the pattern yarns because I think it makes for a neater finish. The tapestry rather than the regular plain weave was used because it helps to establish the rug to its full width from the beginning.

FRINGE

After the 1½ inches of hem, long pile was attached to the warp with Ghiordes knots to form a fringe across the rug, beginning with the first end to the left and ending with the last end. In order to continue the line of the zigzag stripe which the design was to form, each fringe knot was made of the color of the stripe it ended. Two picks of filling were inserted and the design begun. The fringe at the end of the rug was inserted after the last pattern row and 2 picks of plain weave, and made with a reverse Ghiordes knot (see page 53).

PATTERN "STITCH"

Three-stranded butterflies were made for each of the jagged "stripes" of the design. The work was begun from the left-hand side of the rug by inserting the end of the first butterfly in the loop of the first Ghiordes knot to secure it in place, and at the same time to become part of the fringe. This and all other butterflies could

127

have been so secured at the same time the fringe was being knotted, but it would have been confusing to work with so many ends; so they were later pulled through with a crochet hook as each separate butterfly came up, and an extra tug of the knot given to tighten them up again. The yarn was then inserted from the right of and under the first end; and from the right of and under the second end, coming to the surface above the loop formed by the crossing of the yarn, ready to go in the opposite direction in the next row. Like the tapestry technique, each succeeding butterfly was inserted within its own area so that it worked in the opposite direction from those adjacent to it. To follow it through a bit more: the second butterfly end was pulled into the fifth fringe knot, and the yarn then inserted from the left of and under the tenth

warp end; and from the left of and under the third warp end, coming to the surface above the loop of the stitch. The third butterfly end was pulled through the loop of the sixth fringe knot, and the yarn inserted from the right of and under the eleventh warp end; and from the right of and under the eighteenth warp end, coming to the surface above the loop of the stitch. And so on across the row. Maximum advantage of the pattern yarn was taken by crossing it back and forth on the surface of the rug instead of bringing it over and under the warp ends within its motif.

Two picks of bubbled plain weave were inserted between all pattern rows, the maximum which in this case would fit yet not show on the surface of the rug.

The pattern rows were worked alternately from left to right and then right to

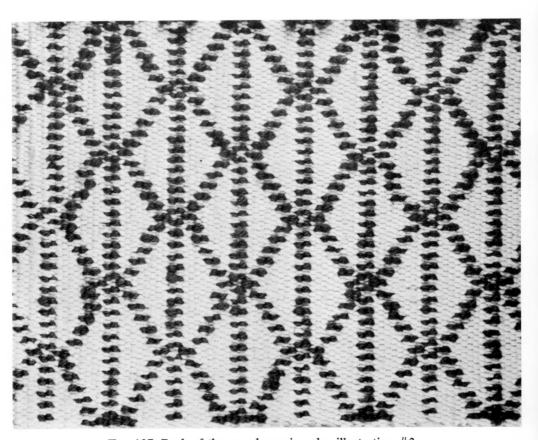

FIG. 107. Back of the rug shown in color illustration #3.

left. In each succeeding pattern row the yarn was crossed from one side to the other, going over and under the last warp end of its motif. On the diagonal side of the motif, every other pattern row, one yarn picked up one end while the other yarn dropped one end. It is interesting to note from the illustration that the dovetailing which occurs in the diagonal line is the same as that of the tapestry diagonal line.

As at the beginning of the rug, the ends of the pattern yarn were pulled into the loop of the fringe knot and cut off as part of the fringe. The rug was finished with rug tape dyed the same color as the filling yarn.

WARP CLOTH FOUNDATION

Since the soumak and this latter technique are applied rather than woven into a fabric, they too, like the knotted pile, could be stitched onto a foundation fabric already woven, such as warp cloth or other sturdy type fabric.

CHAPTER 13

Double Cloth Rugs

The thickness of double cloth which, as its name implies, consists of two separate cloths—an upper or face fabric, and a lower or back fabric—makes it a heavy, durable one which can be used for rugs. In order to be able to weave 2 separate fabrics, each layer of cloth must have its own warp and filling, and each warp must be drawn into its own set of harnesses. Since each layer works independently of the other, then, the weave used for the face fabric can be different from or the same as the back fabric; not that differing weaves are of any great value for hand-loomed rugs, unless one acts as a backing for a favorite face weave which by itself would be too flimsy.

The simplest of the weaves, the plain weave, when used for both sides of the fabric would require at least 2 harnesses for the upper cloth and at least 2 harnesses for the lower cloth, a total of 4 harnesses. If the same warp and filling yarns were used for each side of the fabric, the warp would be made up with double the number of ends required for one layer, and the ends would be drawn into the harnesses so that they alternate one for the upper fabric, the next for the lower fabric. If they were drawn into the harnesses in a straight sequence of 1, 2, 3, 4 and all odd ends were the upper fabric warp, the ends in odd harnesses 1 and 3 would interlace with all odd picks to construct the

upper fabric; the even ends entered into even harnesses 2 and 4 would interlace with all even picks to construct the lower fabric.

When harnesses 1 and 3 are alternately raised to form the upper fabric, there is no problem—the lower fabric ends have remained below where they belong. If harnesses 2 and 4 came up separately above the ends of harnesses 1 and 3, both fabrics would become incorporated into one thick cloth. So that the top fabric ends will always remain on top where they belong while the lower fabric ends are interlacing with their picks, harnesses 1 and 3 must be raised along with the alternate raising of harnesses 2 and 4. Fig. 108A shows a cross section of what happens in the first vertical repeat, or first 4 picks of the plain weave double cloth. Four horizontal repeats are pictured to show more clearly what goes on.

No. 1 in Fig. 108A shows the sequence of upper and lower fabric ends and the harnesses in which they have been drawn. No. 2 shows which ends are up and which are down in the order in which each of the 4 picks forming a repeat of the weave is inserted. The 16 ends in No. 3 are assumed to be the full width of the fabric to show the relationship of the ends and the filling during a pick-by-pick building up of the fabric in one repeat of the weave. No. 4 shows one repeat of the weaving draft, reading from top to bottom (in order to coincide with the reading of No. 3), which produces the 2 layers of fabric.

3(d) in Fig. 108A shows clearly that if the weave were continued in this manner a pocket would be formed between the upper and lower layers which eventually would make it a tubular fabric. Even if closed up at both ends by weaving the 2 layers together in a straight plain weave, this construction would not be particularly suitable for a rug. Both layers would gradually slip apart and twist; the rug

would become misshapen, and the added friction due to slippage would cause it to wear more quickly. One of the chief characteristics of double cloth is that the 2 layers are joined together at intervals to hold both in place by one of various combinations of "stitchings" without changing the appearance of either layer. In double cloths for general use, this perhaps is most often done by leaving down a proportion of face warp ends to interlace with a lower fabric pick, by raising a proportion of lower fabric ends to interlace with an upper fabric pick, or by doing both. The

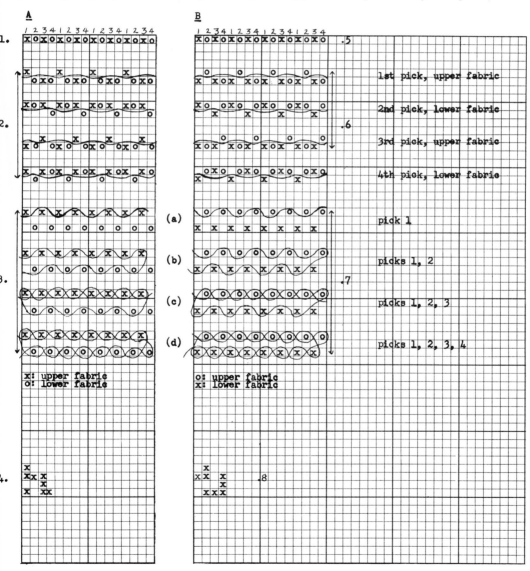

FIG. 108. Double cloth; 4 harnesses; plain weave on both sides.

131

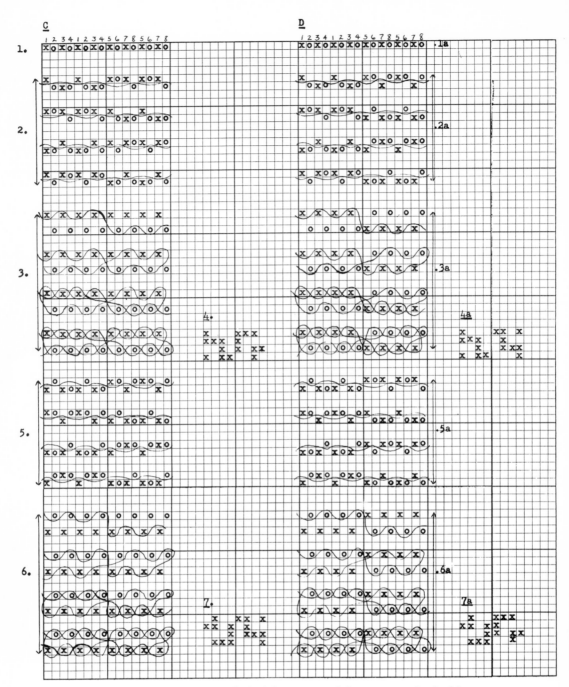

FIG. 109. Double cloth; 8 harnesses; plain weave on both sides.

proportion of warp ends left down or brought up is dependent upon the construction of the upper fabric in relation to the lower fabric. In most cases this type of stitching requires more than one warp beam because the stitching ends take up faster than the others and therefore require different tensioning from the others.

It also increases the number of harnesses by one for each type of stitching end which works differently from other warp ends.

Another type of stitching which requires only one warp beam can be used when both layers of fabric are of exactly the same construction, a feature quite advantageous for rugs since both layers would tend to wear at an equal rate. This method of stitching consists of changing the position of the warp and/or filling threads at intervals so that they alternate in use for both upper and lower fabrics. Stitching the double cloth already discussed and illustrated with this method, then, would consist of completely reversing the position of the warps as shown in Illustration B, Fig. 108, so that what had been the upper warp, ends in harnesses 1 and 3, becomes the lower warp; and what had been the lower warp, ends in harnesses 2 and 4, becomes the upper warp. Nos. 5, 6, and 7 show the change in position of the ends which brings about this transition in a pick-by-pick development of a single repeat of the weave. What actually happens is that the pocket between the 2 layers is horizontally closed up, and another one begun with the warps in complete reverse. In a 4-harness double weave, this stitching or joining can occur only horizontally. No. 8 shows one weaving draft, reading from top to bottom, to bring this about.

The addition of 4 more harnesses makes it possible to have this type of stitching in a vertical as well as a horizontal direction. When sections of the whole warp are alternately drawn into the first 4 harnesses and then into the last 4, the ends drawn into harnesses 1–4 can weave independently of the ends in harnesses 5–8. One pick can then be made to weave the upper fabric of the harnesses 1–4 section while it is weaving the lower fabric of the harnesses 5–8 section. The next pick would, of course, weave the lower fabric of harnesses 1–4, and the upper fabric of harnesses 5–8.

This can be achieved by reversing the position of the picks only, or by reversing the position of the ends and the picks. Fig. 109(C) shows how this is done when changing only the position of the filling. No. 1 shows the sequence of upper and lower fabric ends and the harnesses in which they have been drawn. No. 2 shows which ends are up and which are down

in the order in which each of the 4 picks forming a repeat of the weave is inserted. The 16 ends in No. 3 are assumed to be the full width of the fabric to show the relationship of the ends and the filling during a pick-by-pick building up of the fabric in one repeat of the weave. No. 4 shows one repeat of the weaving draft, reading from top to bottom, which produces the 2 layers of fabric. No. 5 shows one repeat, pick by pick, which achieves, in this set-up, the horizontal closure through reversal of upper and lower warps as described in Fig. 109(D). No. 6 shows how these 4 picks gradually build up a single repeat of the weave; No. 7 is the weaving draft for No. 6, read from top to bottom.

Fig. 109(D) shows how the vertical and horizontal stitchings are achieved by changing the position of both the ends and the picks, and follows the picks through their simple repeat sequence. It will be noted that the only difference between this and Fig. 109(C) is that the upper warp in both sections of (C) is either all odd ends, or all even ends. In (D), one section of the upper warp is formed by odd ends, while the other section is formed by even ends.

APPLICATION OF DOUBLE CLOTH TO A SPECIFIC RUG (FILLING-FACED)

When picks alternating in color are used with this type of stitching, quite attractive color juxtapositions can be produced through oblongs, squares, and stripes. In order to illustrate how this juxtaposition of color can be practically applied to a rug, the following is a step-by-step description of how the rug of Illustration 5 was made.

The warp was not to show—it was to be completely covered by a filling-faced plain weave—so it was made up of 8-ply cotton cord to be sleyed 16 to the inch, 8 for the upper warp and 8 for the lower warp. The color oblongs were to be the same on both edges of the rug and were planned to be uneven in number so this could happen. The outer oblongs were to be 4 inches wide, and the 5 inner ones $3\frac{1}{2}$ inches wide, a full width of $25\frac{1}{2}$ inches. The warps for the 2 layers of the rug were made simultaneously, the full width of the warp having 408 ends ($25\frac{1}{2}$ inches wide x 8 ends per inch = 204 ends for one layer, x 2 for both layers = 408 ends). Only a single warp beam was needed because the 2 sides of the rug were to be of exactly the same construction with the same cotton warp and the same Persian rug wool filling.

The ends were drawn from back to front in alternate sections. The 64 ends of the first 4-inch oblong (4 inches x 8 ends per inch x 2 for both fabric layers = 64) were drawn into the first 4 harnesses in a straight sequence of 1, 2, 3, 4. The 56 ends of the next $3\frac{1}{2}$-inch oblong ($3\frac{1}{2}$ inches x 8 ends per inch x 2) were drawn into the last 4 harnesses in a straight sequence of 5, 6, 7, 8. The rest of the warp was drawn in alternate sections in the same manner according to the width of the oblongs. The ends were then sleyed 16 to the inch, tied onto the cloth beam, and the weaving was begun.

The weave used was No. 4 alternating with No. 7 of Fig. 109(C). Three colors were to be used—red purple, deep blue purple, and rust. The rug was started with about $1\frac{1}{2}$ inches of blue purple only, 1 inch of which was to be rolled under later for a hem. Each color was to weave for about an inch but was to be staggered so it would weave next to both of the other 2 colors. Since only 2 colors can alternate in width at one time, the staggering of color was begun, after the $1\frac{1}{2}$ inches of purple, by weaving alternate picks of red purple with blue purple for about a half inch. In the next half inch, the rust replaced the red purple; and in the next half inch the red purple wove alternately with the rust, etc., on to the finish of the rug. The rug was finished with $1\frac{1}{2}$ inches of purple to correspond to the

beginning of the rug. To close up the pockets at the edges of the rug (otherwise there would have been two flaps), each pick was interlocked with the preceding pick before being inserted into its shed.

In this case, where the filling completely covered the warp, the horizontal stitching resulting from the alternate use every 3 inches of weaving sequences No. 4 and No. 7 of Fig. 109(C) contributed only toward the construction of the fabric. The design could have been exactly the same if this stitching had not been used, but there would have been vertical pockets the length of the rug and these would have been subject to wear from friction due to slippage.

The rug was finished by square-knotting one upper layer with one lower layer warp end all across the warp. About an inch of the purple woven for hems at either end was turned under and rolled into a hem. The hem was held in place by sewing fringe just above it, and knotting it as close to the ends of the rug as possible.

REGULAR PLAIN WEAVE

In the rug just described, the warp, because it was covered by the filling, played no part in the coloring of the rug. If one desired to make a rug with both warp and filling showing, solid blocks and stripes of color could still occur, but the warp would have to be colored as well as the filling. In order for this to happen, the filling and the warp being woven together must both be the same color. Since the filling can weave only in 2 positions— alternately with the upper fabric and with the lower fabric—only 2 solid color blocks or stripes can occur. For instance, black filling can weave alternately with a black upper warp and a black lower warp, while white filling weaves alternately with juxtaposed white lower and white upper warps to form solid color areas. If the black ends are drawn in so that they are all on odd harnesses, and the white ends are drawn in so that they are all on even harnesses, as they are shown in Fig. 109(D) (assuming that in No. 1a the blacked-in squares represent black ends and the circled squares represent white ends), weave No. 4a will produce alternate areas of all black and all white if picks are alternated one black with one white. Continuing with weave No. 4a would produce stripes. Changing to weave No. 7a would reverse the position of the warps and therefore the position of the solid color blocks, provided the filling were also reversed to one white alternating with one black pick. In other words, the one black to the one white ratio of picks would have to be interrupted at the transition point to reverse the position of the picks—the last pick in the repeat of weave No. 4a and the first pick in the repeat of weave No. 7a would both be white picks.

The same result could be achieved by using weaves Nos. 4 and 7 of Fig. 109(C). In this case, the picks would remain static—one black to one white—whereas the ends would have to be reversed by drawing them one black, one white in harnesses 1, 2, 3, 4, but changing their positions in harnesses 5–8 to 1 white, 1 black. This would result in 2 adjacent ends of the same color at the junction point of each warp section.

This does not preclude the inclusion of other colors in the warp and filling, but doing so will result in another effect. Where the same colors weave together, the blocks would be solid, where the colors differ the effect would be a blend, an effect not to be scoffed at but rather to be considered. The decision of which method to use will be up to the weaver.

CHAPTER 14

Filling-Faced Rugs

The same principle of juxtaposition of color areas can be produced with a single cloth in which the warp is completely covered by the filling as described in the previous chapter. For lack of a better term it shall be referred to as **FILLING-FACED**, although many other rugs, including tapestry and soumaks, fall into the same category. In fact, the setting of the warp is the same as that of the tapestry rug because the filling must have room enough to pack down.

In this system, 2 picks of different colors weave exactly the opposite of one another. Assuming these colors to be black and white, what happens is that the first, the black pick, goes over and under certain ends and the next, the white pick, does just the opposite by going under and over the same series of ends. When these picks are continued in the same order, the face of the rug is a play of black against white with just the reverse underneath. The play of color can be varied in any number of ways by changing the combinations of ends coming up, thus creating new effects and motifs. The number of combinations possible depends upon the number of harnesses available and upon the manner in which the ends have been drawn into the harnesses. There is no limit to the number of colors that can be introduced to form either very subtle gradings

of color areas or to form very bold ones with abrupt changes.

Fig. 110 shows a sample of but a few of the combinations of effects and motifs that can be produced by the use of this system with just 2 filling colors when the ends have been drawn into the harnesses in straight rotation. Each of these could be a potential for an integral part of a rug design. Looking at them from the bottom up:

1. A plain weave with black picks alternating with white. The 2 upper bands show how this looks when the positions of the 2 colors are reversed. The reversal is done by interrupting the pick for pick rhythm and inserting 2 picks of one color in succession.

2. A plain weave with 2 picks of black alternating with 2 picks of white to form a wavy pattern.

3. The same as #1, with the positions of the colors changing more often. Whereas #1 looks more like a continuation of staggered stripes, the stripes in this one seem to have been divided into 2 separate sets of vertically jagged horizontal stripes. This is because in changing the position of the colors 2 picks of black were used each time in #1; in #2, 2 picks of white were used to change the position a

136

FIG. 110. Sampler of filling-faced motifs and effects.

137

FIG. 111. Jute background, ramie Ghiordes-knotted pile rug. The background was done with filling-faced effect as #4 in Fig. 110; the pile with Ghiordes knots. Rug made and photographed in Taiwan.

second time, thus breaking the continuity of the black line and separating each "stripe" into 2 motifs. Had more white picks been woven than just the 2 necessary to change the color positions, a more defined break would, of course, have occurred. All of the first 3 could be done on a 2-harness loom.

4. A variation on themes 1 and 2, the first section weaving alternating single picks of black and white in a 2-up, 2-down combination of harness raising; the second portion is 2 picks of black alternating with 2 white in the same 2-up, 2-down harness combination; the third portion is the plain weave of #1 repeated here simply to show how contrast in size looks.

The first 2 portions of this could be done on a 2-harness loom with 2 ends drawn into the first harness alternating with 2 ends drawn into the second harness. But, once the loom was set up that way, of course, it would be impossible to get the 1-up, 1-down harness combination of the third portion. The combination of all 3 would require 4 harnesses.

5. A 3-up, 1-down variation of #3 done on a 4-harness loom. White picks weave in the harnesses 1, 2, 3 up, 4 down shed alternating with black picks weaving in the harnesses 1, 2, 3 down, 4 up shed; the alternation of verticals is a change of weave to black picks in harnesses 1, 3, 4 down, 2 up shed alternating with white picks in harnesses 1, 3, 4 up, 2 down shed.

6. A series of stripes of the plain weave of #1, closed at the bottoms and tops

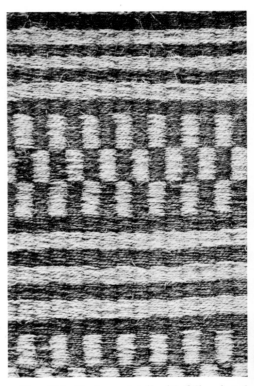

FIG. 112. Sisal rug detail with filling-faced effects. Done on a tatami loom. Made and photographed in Taiwan.

to form oblongs by weaving a few picks (in this case 6) of the weave used in the upper portion of #5.

7. Practically the same as #6 except that, instead of forming oblongs, the upper closing alternates with the bottom closing to form a fret or Greek key design. Since the bottom closing was formed by weaving black picks in a shed with harnesses 1, 3, 4 down, 2 up and white picks in the opposite shed of 1, 3, 4 up, 2 down, then, in order to alternate, the top closing must weave black picks in a shed with harnesses 1, 2, 3 down, 4 up and white picks in a 1, 2, 3 up, 4 down shed. Outline the whole with white and you have the basis for a rug motif.

8. Plain weave with 4 picks of black alternating with 1 white, 1 black, 1 white. The second portion is the same repeat of picks widened out to 2 ends up, 2 ends down.

9. A crosslike motif formed by changing the positions of the colors in a 2-up, 2-down harness combination. The upper one is slightly bigger because more white picks were inserted. The whole is surrounded by plain weave with black only.

This group is merely a beginning in a long list of possible combinations with just a straight draw. Using pointed or sectional draws, and more than just 2

Fig. 113. Detail of a contemporary sisal rug with filling-faced effects. Fringe of jute made with Ghiordes and reversed Ghiordes knots. Taiwanese photograph. (Courtesy of *Handweaver and Craftsman* magazine.)

colors, would increase the possibilities that much more. You are urged to make samplers of your own, trying out various draws and seeing how various colors affect one another when so juxtaposed. It could be rewarding—such exploration often leads to creative discovery.

MISCELLANEOUS

CHAPTER 15

Oval, Circular, or Nonrectilinear Rugs

It is not necessary to design only rectilinear rugs for production on a handloom; it is quite possible to make other shapes.

When such a rug is to be made, design the rug as usual, making a full-scale model of it on stiff paper. Place the model on the warp, leaving enough room for a hem if one is desired; a hem will be necessary in the case of a pile rug in order to hold the edge knots or tufts in place. Trace the design of the rug onto the warp, including the outer contours of the rug; measure and mark outer contours of the hem. Instead of measuring, a separate paper model can be made of the bigger shape only, if desired. The model of the shape alone for transfer purposes need be no more than half the size of the rug—it can be flipped over for the other side of the rug. If these shapes are of a size to be repeated often, it might be advisable to make the models of something more durable than stiff paper—Bristol board, cardboard, or thin plywood. Except for aesthetic reasons, no hem is necessary along the straight sides of an oval rug; the edges are of good construction if finished like rectangular or square rugs. Not so in the circular rugs since there are no straight edges—the hem should continue all the way around. When making up a warp for a rug with a hem all around, enough extra ends must be added to both sides to take care of the width of the hem desired.

WEAVING THE RUG

If weaving were done only within the contours of an oval or circular rug, ignoring the rest of the warp and just letting it be, the edges would start sagging toward the free warp space, the rug would gradually become misshapen, and weaving problems would begin. In order to avoid this and the bad construction which would be the result, the edges of the rounded contours can be supported and held in place by one of the following methods:

1. By weaving the filling across the full width of the warp and cutting off the excess after the rug is taken off the loom. It is advisable to sew rug tape on by machine along the edge of what will be the hem before rather than after cutting off excess to prevent any unnecessary raveling. The hem can then be turned under and stitched like rectilinear rugs.

2. By the tapestry method. The method of weaving in this case will be the same as that for weaving the circular or elliptical shapes described in the Tapestry Rug section on page 113. Three parts will have to be working separately: (a) the left side and (b) the right side of the warp which will not form a part of the rug; and (c) the center section, or the rug itself. Since the weaving with the (a) and

143

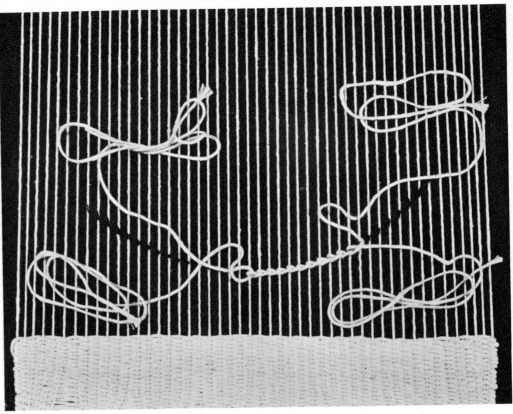

FIG. 114. Twining at the bottom or beginning of an oval-contoured rug.

(b) filling shuttles merely acts as support which will later be discarded, it does not need to be woven as carefully as the rug, nor does it have to be woven pick for pick with it. It needs only to be inserted often enough to keep the rug supported and woven in a straight horizontal line. Using a heavier filling yarn than the rug's, without bubbling it, will cut down on the number of supporting picks required. The quality of the filling yarn for these sections is unimportant since it does not form part of the rug. Needless to say, when the rug reaches its full width, there is no further need for the supporting sections.

When the other end of the rug is reached, the curve changes position and the rug starts getting smaller rather than bigger. The edges cannot sag because the main body of the rug now acts as support, but they can loosen up. It may be found helpful particularly in

finishing the rug, or even necessary, if about an inch or so of weaving next to the hem is continued now and then to help keep the picks in place. The rug can be finished in one of the ways discussed under "Finishing the Woven Rug," page 50.

3. By using the twining process. Unless the warp ends are spaced too far apart, this is a very good system when a hand beater is being used. Depending upon what kind of warp yarn is used in relation to the twining yarn, and how close the warp ends are, this method may or may not work at the beginning of a rug when a horizontal beater is used— it will definitely work at the end of such a rug. To do this, you will need 2 lengths of cotton cord each about 2½ to 3 times as long as the outside rounded contour of the section of the rug being outlined. Insert one length of cord at its center underneath one of the center ends of the warp so that

144

both ends of the cord go toward the left; insert the other length at its center, linking it around the first length of cord, and underneath the same center warp end so that both ends of cord go toward the right. With a twist of the cord working toward the left, bring the end of cord coming from underneath the warp end over the other end of cord and insert it from the left of, under and around to the right of the next warp end, bringing it completely around that warp end on the surface of the warp and toward the weaving; pick up the other end of cord, bringing it over the cord end just dropped, and insert it from the left of, under and around to the right of the next warp end, bringing it completely around that warp end on the surface of the warp and toward the weaving; continue twining firmly and tightly in this manner, but without pulling, first with one end of the cord and then with the next, following the contours of the outer edge of the hem. The same procedure is followed with the cord going to the right, except that the direction of the movement is reversed—the end of cord goes from the right of and under the next warp end, emerging on the surface from the left of that warp end.

The twining at the beginning of the rug can be done all at once or gradually along with the weaving of the rug; the principle is the same as for sectional weaving in the tapestry technique. It has to be done gradually at the end of the rug. Finish the rug as desired. If the warp is used as fringe, twining should be sufficient to hold it in place without the necessity for further warp knotting. Thus, the weaver saves time and effort.

CHAPTER 16

Aids to the Planning or Designing of Rugs

There are only 3 elements entering into the actual making of a rug: material or yarn, technique, and color. No rug can be made using more than these, and no rug can be made without using all 3. Yet a design is present even when these 3 are used in their simplest possible combination of one yarn, one variation of a technique, and one color to form a plain rug. An arrangement of the details making up the rug has taken place which by definition constitutes a design. And, consciously or unconsciously, the person who planned the rug has begun to design because he has participated in forming that pattern. He has had to make a choice between which one yarn (soft or wiry, thick or thin, lustrous or dull), which one technique (looped or cut pile, low and velvety or high and shaggy; the ribbed tapestry or the stitch-raised soumak), and which one color (light or dark, neutral or bright) will be used above all others. If it is a woven rug, he has had to set the warp to a certain number of ends per inch; insert the knots or loops, if a pile rug, at certain intervals in the weaving; and beat the filling in firmly to form a certain density.

Most of us, however, are not satisfied with making plain rugs alone. We want to express ourselves somehow by breaking up the expanse of plain space in an interesting way with some sort of line, theme, or motif. Various methods can be used to develop such motifs, such as drawing on paper or cutting out paper shapes, but the only way the lines of those developed motifs can be introduced or translated to rug form is through a contrast in at least one of the weaving elements. This contrast furnishes the lines of demarcation which delineate the planned motifs; it need not furnish the impetus for the design idea, however. The motif often comes to mind first, the contrast not coming into play until the means of translation must be chosen in order to start the rug. Ideas come from all sorts of sources within and outside ourselves, quite independently of the rug-making process. The spark of an idea for a rug is often set off by seeing a leaf, a shadow, cracks in the sidewalk, sun-drenched colors of a weather-beaten tin can . . . even when no rug is being contemplated. How design ideas come to us and how we go about arranging them into a coordinated whole is so entirely personal that one can only suggest possible avenues of thought or observation which might be stimulants for the generation of ideas, their treatment and arrangement into rug designs.

Since the rug-making elements are immutable and so much an integral part of the design, getting to know them and to understand how they can be used as tools to interpret specific effects or moods is extremely important in reaching the goal of satisfyingly good design. The benefits derived from exploring the process, and some methods of doing so will therefore be discussed first. Many suggestions for treatment of design ideas have already been made under the sections covering each technique. A review of those sections considered in the light of what follows will undoubtedly be found helpful.

SAMPLE WARPS

Using sample warps is one of the best ways to become acquainted with the rug-making process. As its name implies, a sample warp is usually made only wide enough to accommodate narrow samples; it can be as narrow as 6 inches or as wide as 12 or more inches. It allows the beginner to practice the entire process of a technique more often and, therefore, to get to know it faster than would be possible with a wide warp. It gives him the freedom to experiment with the process as much or as long as he wants to or feels he needs to before going on to the discipline of an actual rug. It enables him to find out how flexible the techniques are, how various warp and filling yarns behave, how colors react in relation to one another, what effect various types of yarns have on the textural quality of a rug. In short, it familiarizes him as nothing else could with the whole of the process and extends his weaving horizons. Thus he has more resources to draw on when an idea begs to be translated to an actual rug.

A sample warp is an invaluable tool which never outgrows its usefulness. The need for exploring is not limited to the beginner; the veteran weaver needs it too. It is through exploring and experimenting that ideas are often generated for a design. There are many times when an idea presents itself which cannot become a reality until it is worked out on the loom.

The sample warp is not only useful for exploratory purposes. When no previous sampling has been done, it can serve as a link between the mental image and the actual rug when a design is not to be conveyed to paper but developed directly on the loom; or between the already finished paper model of the design and the actual rug. Before beginning the rug, in either case, it is wise to try out a representative section or sections of it where changes of color, technique, or texture will be required. It enables one to actually visualize what the rug will look like when finished—a mental or paper image is not always accurate in practicality. The little time it takes to make the sample is well spent—it avoids later disappointment and a possible need for the ripping out of undesired effects.

The nature of the design will determine the size necessary for a useful sample. If the design is composed of a small pattern repeating itself all over, a sample only big enough to show 2 or 3 repeats in both directions is needed; if the design is a single unit with areas of various types of changes, even more than one sample may be needed (if the types of change vary appreciably from one another), each sample big enough to show only a small area of each section where there is a concentration of variation.

These comments also apply to hooked and other rugs whose surfaces are applied to an already woven foundation fabric, in which case the tool for sampling would naturally be a piece of foundation cloth.

There is one thing that must be remembered when making woven samples: the narrower the warp, the more firmly the sample will weave. Allowances for this will have to be made in the rug itself or the design will be distorted. For instance: if in the sample it was necessary to insert 6 picks of filling between knots in a pile rug in order to get a planned 3 rows of knots per vertical inch, in the actual rug it may be necessary to reduce the picks to 5 or 4 in order to get the same proportions.

PILE RUG TECHNIQUE VARIANTS

Illustrated Use of Sample Warp

An excellent way to use the sample warp (or foundation cloth) as an exploratory tool to build up a repertoire of design effects, or even complete designs, is by conducting a series of exercises or experiments of your own. Let us follow an illustration of how this might work, using only technique as a contrast and the plain rug as a starting point. This may be helpful in setting a foundation upon which you could begin to develop your own experiments toward exploring the rug-weaving elements.

Assuming that the plain rug in question is cut pile and that the first contrast introduced is another height of cut pile, its new dimension makes it possible to form stripes—horizontal or vertical, even or uneven in width; shaped motifs—blocks, squares, florals, with straight or curved contours—in low relief (low pile motif surrounded by high pile ground), or in high relief (high pile motif surrounded by low pile background). With the addition of a third cut pile height, these motifs can be done in both high and low relief scattered in a pattern repeated evenly throughout the rug, superimposed upon one another, or arranged as a single unit. The inclusion of other heights of looped or cut pile carries the multiplication of possibilities further, because there is the latitude of still another dimension.

Introduction of looped pile furnishes a new yarn texture and another shade of a color, without having added another kind of yarn or a different shade of color. Where only the velvety surface of the cut yarn was present, there is now the smooth texture of the looped pile. The smooth surface of the loop reflects more light than does the velvety surface of the cut pile which disperses the light because it penetrates and becomes saturated into the core of the fiber—with the result that the looped pile is a lighter, brighter shade than the cut pile which is fuller and deeper in tone.

Included among the many other effective and useful contrasts in pile technique for interpretation of design themes are areas of dense and sparse pile, combinations of pile with flat weaves, and experimental treatment of the basic knots.

FLAT RUG TECHNIQUE VARIANTS

A whole series of exploratory warps could be set up on the basis of suggestions already made in the sections covering each rug type. The varying structures of the rug weaves call for different treatment of contrasts. In flat rugs, where the design depends upon the weave for motifs, contrast in technique is obtained through various interlacing combinations of the warp with the filling. Since the filling yarn must go from one side to the other of the rug with each pick, the contrasts in relative placement of warp and filling can be controlled only by the raising and lowering of warp ends in various combinations. Falling in this category are floated-filling, floated-pile, and double-weave rugs. Samples of technique exploration in these types would consist of trying various combinations of harness raising along with different draws. The floated-filling rug has a multitude of possibilities with various types of draws such as the pointed ones in which the ends might be drawn into a harness sequence of 1, 2, 3, 2; or 1, 2, 3, 4, 3, 2.

The floated pile seems to straddle the rug categories, but its structural properties are those of the flat weave. It, however, has 2 sets of filling yarns with which one can experiment—the pile and the supporting one. Changes in interlacing depend not only upon the draw, but also upon the frequency of the use of pile picks in comparison to plain weave picks. Striped, spotted, squared, and other effects can be achieved through certain placements of pile picks.

Although the tapestry and soumak weaves are flat, they do not depend upon interlacings of warp and filling for delineation of their motifs. Because their surface yarns can change in color, texture, or line at every point where there is an end (a minimum of two ends in the soumak), their motif possibilities are those of knotted or looped pile. Strangely enough, no variation in the one-over, one-under weave structure can take place in the tapestry rug or it would become something else. The main technique variant of the soumak is the size of its stitch. Or is it? Consider the rug discussed on page 126.

It is quite obvious from the foregoing that treatment of designs can take many forms by using technique alone as a contrasting agent. But color, and yarn also, must be allowed to play their roles before design translation can be explored or exploited to its richest and fullest. Yarn has already been discussed (page 12) so it needs no further elaboration.

Color as the Variant

Color is the most flexible of the weaving elements, and is certainly used much more frequently than the other 2 as the dominant—and often the only—interpretive feature of the rug. A great deal of the delight of planning and making rugs comes from the use of color; without it, most rugs would be rather dull and uninteresting to make. Color alone could serve as the agent of design interpretation for most rugs—it does so almost exclusively in the tapestry rug—without ever relying upon technique or yarn except to serve as the instruments for its display. Color contrasts without number are quite possible because another color or shade of a color can always be added, whereas there is a limit to the number of pile heights, for instance, that could be combined in a single rug. To say nothing of the confusion which that many pile heights would cause! Too many colors can be confusing, however. It is not the number but rather the manner of treating it which makes

color an effective tool. An economy of color, deftly used, can produce extremely successful rugs.

Each of the elements has the advantages of its own properties, however, and the person making the rug should not deprive himself of them. Getting the best use out of all 3 in a given situation is the ideal one looks for in good design. Not all designs should be executed alike—certain moods or feelings will demand that color shall dominate, and others that all 3 elements be equally meshed together. The best way to find the happy integration of all 3 is to make samples, either exploratory ones before beginning to work on the graphic element of the design; or confirmatory ones after the design is completed. There is a certain dimensional quality achieved through pile heights, for instance, which can never be duplicated with color alone, even though it can be approximated by the use of strong contrasts, such as a white motif on a black background, or vice versa. The white in the first instance tends to pop up visually, and the black in the second to recede. A sample will help determine which dimensional quality expresses the mood of the rug more effectively—color in strong contrast; or, that of 2 more closely allied colors or 2 shades of the same color in combination with 2 heights of pile, with 2 yarn sizes in the tapestry rug, or with 2 sizes of stitch in the soumak. Or, which most closely fits the mental visualization of the idea to be conveyed—the all-cut pile of 2 closely related shades of one color, or the contrast and textural quality achieved by looped and cut pile of the same color. In fact, 2 or 3 colors in both looped and cut pile can give the illusion that a much larger number of colors has been used. An economy of color!

But, even before this kind of thinking goes on, there may be a doubt in some people's minds as to how to begin to think in terms of color at all. Telling or suggesting to anyone how to do this is difficult, if not almost impossible. Use of color is an emotional and psychological experience rather than one which appeals to reason; some people like certain colors to which others have a strong aversion. Color does not lend itself to rules. It is another of those intangibles which one can only feel for himself, and for which the person planning the rug is his own best judge. He should use colors he likes and enjoys working with. They should be carefully planned and arranged so that they enrich rather than impoverish one another, and so that they properly relate to the other colors in the area in which the rug is to be placed. The knowledge of whether colors enrich or vitalize one another can come only by acquainting oneself with color through experimenting with it, learning to observe it, and having the courage to use it as one sees and enjoys it. Some people have a flair or an instinct for color which can guide them to the proper choices. Others are either less sensitive to it or are a bit timid about asserting themselves in its use. For those people, it might be of help to state that the wide range of contrasts possible through the use of color as a design translation agent can be broken down to 2 types: monochromatic and polychromatic. Monochromatic contrasts involve the use of 2 or more tones of the same color, such as 2 or 3 tones of green. Those tones can be light and lighter; dark and darker; light and dark; or light, medium, and dark. Polychromatic constrasts involve the use of colors that differ from one another. Those colors can be neighboring ones such as orange and yellow and their various in-between tones, or direct opposites such as red and green and their various neighboring tones, in the rainbow or spectrum sequence of what is generally referred to as red, orange, yellow, green, blue, violet. Actually, there are innumerable gradations of colors in between each so that no change from one to the other as we name it is perceptible. Brought one small step further, this sequence would be red, red-orange, orange, orange-yellow, yellow,

yellow-green, green, green-blue, blue, and blue-violet. The neighboring ones are generally considered to be harmonies of analogy, and the opposing colors complementary or harmonies of contrast. The tones of colors within those combinations which best relate to one another must still be chosen—the yellow, for instance, in the yellow-green of a green, yellow-green and blue-green analogous harmony might be too strong and rob the other colors of their quality. Such pinpointing of the broad realm of color into harmoniously considered combinations should not be considered a rule; it is merely a guide to make it easier for some people to find a starting point from which to proceed to develop a color scheme.

Becoming more inquisitive about color can greatly increase your knowledge of how to use it. Since nature is all around us, and since it furnishes the various lights without which no color could exist, learn to use it as one of your observation points about color. Notice, for instance, how colors change as the quality and intensity of light changes—on a humid summer day and a clear one; on a crisp winter day and a storm-clouded one. Notice how much more exciting colors are in the morning and early afternoon than they are at the height of the midday sun. The shadows that enrich the contrasts between colors during early morning and late afternoon are almost nonexistent at midday so that colors become washed out like an overexposed film. Is this not the same effect that two colors of the same light value and low intensity have upon one another, such as pale blue and pale green—that they "do" nothing for one another? But, when a deeper green, blue, or blue-green is added they both become more alive? Or—if one looks at a desert or an arid area long enough, one can usually begin to see the varying shades that made up the plain beige of 5 or 10 minutes ago —the pink, the gray, the green tones in the beige—so that a kaleidoscope of color is present. Subtle, but nonetheless dramatic in its understatement. Even a color scheme based on neutrals can be quite colorful and at the same time quite restful.

Colors interlaced into a weave have a different relationship to one another than in a free-standing pile. The interlacing of one color with another can reduce the value of a strong color which will merely stand out as raw in a pile rug. On the other hand, a raw color used as accent rather than as a large area can be just the touch needed in a particular rug. A color juxtaposed to another can be something very different when those two colors are separated by a third color; a brighter green can bring out mostly the gray of a soft green, whereas a more neutral-toned color will emphasize its soft green quality. Colors can be made to vibrate if used in proper combination. This is more apt to happen satisfactorily in dark shades such as black and blue, black and deep red purple, olive and a deep russet, or olive and a deep blue-green.

But, these comparisons are all relative because a precise method of communication about color is lacking—what is blue-green to one is green to another, and blue to still another; what is raw to one is almost mellow to another, and so on. As time goes on, experimentation and observation can help you set up or increase your own vocabulary of color. You are its best judge.

DEVELOPING THE THEME OR MOTIF OF THE DESIGN

How one proceeds to develop the design for a rug depends much upon the person and the circumstances at the time, as well as upon the technique that will be used. The few types of flat rugs discussed in this book that rely on the weave for the theme or motif are often best approached on the loom, as are certain types of textural and small-motifed designs for pile rugs. We are here more concerned with designs whose scale of repeat is either too big to sketch completely on the loom or on warp cloth as an actual sample, or which are more like prints.

The following must be regarded merely as guides or suggestions, not as rules, and not as a specific order of procedure. Perhaps no rug is approached exactly in the same way as was the one previous to it. The spark can be set off in a number of ways—by a beautiful color or yarn one time, by an idea for a motif another time. Only the germ of an idea might be present, or its mental conception might be very clear. Whatever the sequence or stage of thoughts preliminary to the decision to make a rug, there are certain considerations one should take into account when planning it. How big should the rug be to properly complete the area in which it is to be placed? What shape? What function is the rug to have—is it to be an accent rug—one that is easy to live with no matter what one's mood—or is it just an idea begging to be tried out? What should be its coloring—neutrals?—bright colors?—is it to coordinate with a present decor or to be the basis around which a color scheme for the room or area is later to be formed? What technique is to be used? Once you have decided what shape and size the rug is to be and what technique is to be used, you are ready to start developing its theme.

Unless the design is to be a small-patterned overall repeat, it is usually advisable to cut a heavy brown paper model the actual size and shape the rug is to be for use as the basis for the development of your design. This makes it possible to plan the shapes and their sizes, the width of stripes, etc., and their placement in proper relationship to the space within the rug's confines, and the space and furniture within the rug's area. The total area of the rug should not look crowded or cluttered, nor should there be so much free space that the design looks skimpy.

How to explain the difference between crowded and well-filled, or skimpy and uncluttered, the writer is at a loss to do.

Fig. 115. Using cutout shapes as a medium for designing. Shapes have been cut in various forms—mass, and in outline. The shapes can be pushed around and placed in various positions until a pleasing design has been developed.

For instance, the full bloom of the bottom section of the Persian rug illustrated on page 14 and the "mille-fleurs" type of design of old, such as in the Unicorn tapestries are rich, not cluttered. Why? These, of course, have a scale of design one cannot afford in time or otherwise to work on in our age. The point is that there is an indefinable something which tells one whether space is treated well, or whether a design is good, for that matter. And who can best judge what is satisfactory treatment of that space but you when you develop your own rug designs? Your paper model cut to size and shape will help you decide when the design is a well-integrated whole that will assert itself, but not intrude on its surroundings.

It is useless to design motifs or shapes the details of which are too complicated to conform readily to the repeat of a "weave" —for instance, the number of knots per inch in a pile rug, the number of ends per inch in a tapestry rug, the number of harnesses you have available for a double-weave rug. So, consider the method you will use carefully before you begin developing its theme. In general, it is best to avoid small detail, and to keep it simple. Then start thinking about the motif. You may already have one in mind—a stripe, a floral, a geometric. Work it out with preliminary sketches in any medium you find easiest—by trailing strands of yarn into lines or shapes and tracing the final result, by drawing or doodling until you

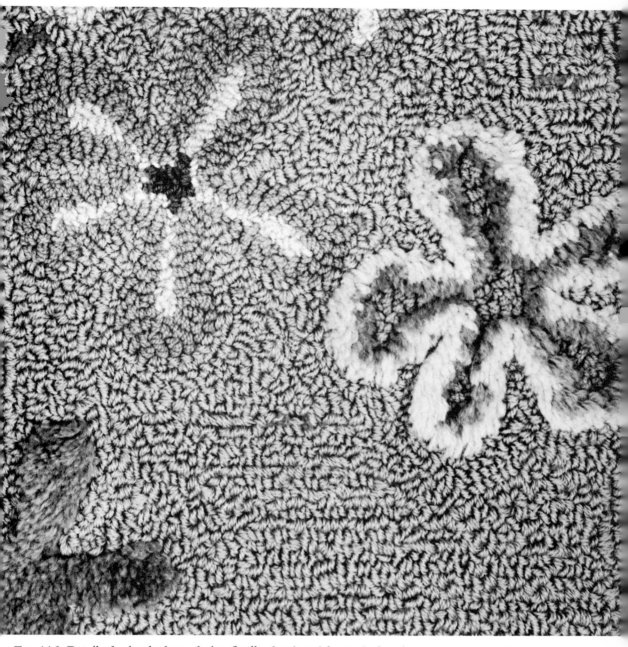

FIG. 116. Detail of a hooked rug design finally developed from placing shapes as shown in Fig. 115. A few heights of pile and textures of yarn are illustrated.

eventually arrive at a motif or motifs pleasing to you. You may do this on the paper rug model, rather lightly at first, if with pencil, because you may want to make changes; or on smaller sheets of paper until you are pleased. Transferal from the smaller sheets can be made by using tracing or carbon paper, or by cutting out. If the motif is to be repeated, make several cutouts of it, in mass form and in outline so that they can be tried in various positions on the model —symmetrically or asymmetrically, in clusters or in regular repeat, with masses and their inside and outside outlines— until you have a composition that satisfies you.

When this happens, trace them carefully onto the model. If the color of the brown model interferes with your visualization of it, color areas of it with wax or pastel-like crayons, spread bunches of the yarn you intend to use within the shapes, or cut out the motifs with colored construction paper. Consider color proportions in relation to one another—they too should not intrude upon, but rather enhance one another. Specific colors can dominate, but they should not domineer.

In choosing colors for your rugs, it is helpful to start with large quantities such as skeins, if possible, rather than snips a few inches long; toss them together on the floor; take out those that don't seem to belong until you have a group that satisfies and pleases you. If it is to be a cut pile rug, bunch together short ends of the colors you have chosen, cut them off evenly, and look into the cut pile to see if it is the combination you want.

Some motifs such as stripes or geometrics can be measured and drawn lightly onto the model until you are sure that the proportions are right for the space within the rug and the whole room or area— space extends beyond itself to its surroundings; or they can be cut out of colored paper and placed on the model until spaced out as you like.

There is no substitute, of course, for sampling portions of the finished design which have the greatest contrast in color or other dominating element on the loom or on foundation cloth, as the case may be, to help you visualize as closely as possible, short of the rug itself, how the finished product will look.

Every part of the rug that is exposed to view should be considered as part of the design of the rug, and the fringes and hems used to finish it treated accordingly. The construction of the rug is also part of the design, even if the eye can't see it. It is part of the function of a rug to be sturdy. A rug design is a good one only when its visual quality and construction are coordinated. A rug beautiful to look at, but badly and loosely put together, lacks an essential quality for which even its attractiveness cannot make up.

SOURCES OF INSPIRATION FOR DESIGN IDEAS

How can one tell another how to go about searching for ideas when they come to each of us in such different ways? When what inspires one will strike absolutely no chord in another? When one can look at something day after day and apparently not be touched by it until, suddenly, it takes on meaning and the germ of an idea is there? There is one method that is bound to work for everyone, and that is the development of a power of observation, if a keen one does not already exist.

Develop an awareness of everyday things—natural and man-made—the play of sunlight on the floor, the texture of a stone wall, the various shadings in a red apple or a green leaf, the way peelings fall from a potato, a slice of fruit cake viewed in the light, fruit and vegetables in cross-section, shadows of clouds and the effect they have on the greens of the trees, the purples in those shadows, the difference in colors under the midday sun and at early evening, details on a building, patterns created by a wrought-iron fence, on fire escapes. . . . Don't make it a

154

chore, don't even search for ideas on some days—just enjoy observing. If you're not receptive today, undoubtedly a picture is being stored in a corner of the brain ready for emergence some day as an idea for a rug design. The more one observes, the more one absorbs and the better the chance for such brain storage.

A good power of observation will help you pick up ideas from the wealth of stimulating material at aquariums, zoos, natural history museums. Rock and shell collections have wonderful surface textures and beautiful color combinations which can generate not only ideas for motifs and how to color them, but also ways of using a technique or texture for interpretation. Nature can teach us so much about how to treat design. So many design patterns in the growth or surfaces of natural forms are the same—the overlapping of feathers in birds' wings, butterfly markings, sea shells, animal horns, reptile skins, patterns on insects, the structure of seed pods, fish scales, pineapple and cactus fruit skins . . . but the variations in the treatment of those design forms!!! Some are raised; some are depressed; they run in stripes, in spirals, in gradations, in spots; some are vividly, even flamboyantly colored; others come in neutrals; they are encrusted, they are glassy smooth; they are velvety, they are prickly; they are symmetrical, they are asymmetrical; their details are clustered, they are scattered. . . . And there are variations within each variation!

Fine arts and decorative arts museums are excellent sources of inspiration. Ideas for color arrangements, forms, textural treatment can be inspired by paintings, sculpture, jewelry, musical instruments, rug and fabric collections, embroideries— both old and contemporary.

Museum libraries and art sections of public libraries have excellent books of photographic blowups of natural forms, of architectural details, sculpture details . . . the treatment and patterns of hair, beards, clothing on cathedral figures have marvelous textural and motif qualities which one could well learn from and adapt to the design of rugs. There are many other types of art and scientific "picture" books from which one can get a fund of ideas. The magnification of the "one drop of water" kind of photos (or a plastic reconstruction in science museums) contains an amazing number of design forms. No source must be either ignored or passed over.

One must not overlook the contemporary scene and this includes "just looking" tours of all kinds of shops to see how color, line, texture are being used in clothing, in glassware and china, in decorative schemes, rugs, furniture. . . . Although we can learn a great deal from the past, we of today, too, have something to contribute. We do that most sincerely when we do not borrow from the past but rather project its reflection into the future through designing within the framework of our own times.

Index

157

MARY ALLARD

is a greatly gifted designer of woven fabrics, wall hangings, and floor coverings, who studied with Lili Blumenau at her studio in New York; at Cranbrook Academy of Art, Bloomfield Hills, Michigan; and at the Lowell Textile Institute, Lowell, Massachusetts.

For many years she has designed fabrics for industry, for yarn manufacturers, and for decorative fabrics and floor-covering manufacturers. Her work has been exhibited at the Detroit Institute of Arts; Cranbrook Academy of Art; the Contemporary Crafts Museum, New York; the "Living Today" exhibit at the Corcoran Gallery of Art, Washington, D. C.; the University of Southern Illinois; and the Good Design exhibition of 1955. In the "Design Derby" in 1957 she received first prize for floor coverings and in the same exhibition in 1962 she was awarded second prize in that category.

Miss Allard has taught at the Fashion Institute of Technology, New York, and has conducted a rug workshop for the York State Craftsmen, in addition to giving private instruction.

A widely traveled woman, always in search of new designs and techniques, Miss Allard has done intensive research in most of the countries of Asia and Europe, and also in Mexico. She was design adviser to the weaving department of a handicraft project under Russel Wright for AID in Taiwan.

Miss Allard now lives and weaves on a quiet street in New York's Greenwich Village.